STAND

TRANSFORM YOUR COMPANY'S HUMAN RESOURCES FROM A GENERIC, LOW-VALUE COMMODITY TO A STRATEGIC SYSTEM THAT FUELS BUSINESS RESULTS

STANDOUT HR

TRANSFORM YOUR COMPANY'S HUMAN RESOURCES FROM A GENERIC, LOW-VALUE COMMODITY TO A STRATEGIC SYSTEM THAT FUELS BUSINESS RESULTS

VERO VANMIDDELEM

For information, contact:
Vero Vanmiddelem
Bekelstraat 137
B-9100 Sint-Niklaas
Belgium

Book and Cover design by 99Designs

First Edition: September 2018

Dedicated to my son

The two most important days in your life are the day you are born and the day you find out why.
—Mark Twain

CONTENTS

ACKNOWLEDGMENTS

When I imagined writing a book, I visualized myself being in a very lonely place, isolated from everyone and everything, immersed in my own feelings and thoughts reflecting solitude, despair, self-doubt but at the same time excitement, desire and flow.

Looking back, I can only say that it was everything but a solitary adventure. I have never felt more surrounded by, supported by, lifted by all those people around me that – all in their own way – managed to add value to my journey.

I have to mention the Self-Publishing School and its Mastermind Community, with Chandler Bolt as CEO, who planted the seeds in me that nothing should hold me back in chasing my dreams, writing about and sharing my passion with the rest of the world.

I had the pleasure of extending my network with specialists, having their heart in the right place and contributing to the success of this 'making of', more specifically my coach Scott Allan, my cover designer Mr. TK at 99designs, and my editor Qat Wanders.

My launch team was awesome. Personal and dear friends, colleagues, and other supportive professionals stood by me, providing me with useful comments and feedback, encouraging me to keep going.

Valerie Schoenfelder was the one who introduced me more than ten years ago to the specific tool I have learned to appreciate, use extensively, and am suggesting in this book as well. I sincerely hope you will discover all the benefits it brings to move HR to the next level.

Finally, I can only praise my luck to have encountered my husband who stands by me ever since he met me more than two decades ago, accepting and supporting all of my crazy endeavors and ideas. I would not have become who I am without him.

My son, the sun in my life, my ever forever treasure, unknowingly stood by me and helped me through my biggest fears and doubts.

I sincerely hope that I can ever give back even a fraction of what I have received.

INTRODUCTION

What does it take for an HR[1] department to contribute positively to your business' results? Have you ever wondered what all the dollars spent on HR initiatives really bring to the table? And why, in other companies, HR investments seem to pay off big, while in your own organization, no matter what, it just doesn't catch on?

How is it that your Chief HR Officer, when asked to demonstrate HR's Return On Investment, wanders off in endless, vague, fluffy, and non-significant prose about how long it takes to see tangible results and about the difficulties in measuring HR impact? HR is not as difficult as that, is it? What is HR—more and other than hiring and firing people, developing them to better contribute to business results while providing them with proper pay and benefits? What else is there to know about HR?

But how is it then that, of all people, high performers resign, while nobody saw it coming? How is it that morale goes down and people fall sick, even when you are partying every third Friday and just managed to bring in a great new project to deliver? How is it that you cannot seem to attract or hire the people you need, although your salary benchmark is top notch?

Standout HR is just what you need and deserve! This book describes what it takes to have HR deliver upon the promise, earning its seat at your C-table[2], not because of the proportion of assets and company resources spent, but because of the impact on your business results.

---

[1] HR is the abbreviation of Human Resources
[2] The C-table is the commonly known term for the management committee, composed of the CEO, CFO, COO, CHRO etc.

HR can only become "Standout," thus contributing maximally to the achievement of your business goals, if it is capable of developing a company-original and embedded HR approach, moving beyond the very basic and generic model that lacks the uniqueness that will boost your business.

I have spent my entire professional life in HR, more than 25 years in multiple roles, multiple companies, and diverse sectors. And in fact, the answer to the above questions is simple. In the end, successful HR is nothing more than applying a simple model.

The in-, through- and outflow model goes back to the basics of HR and will be briefly described in Section 1. This is what can be called generic HR, HR that you see in every organization, without personal touch. No surprises here, and no deep dive either, since there are dozens of books that provide you with the technical basics of HR activities and operations. This first section will give you an overall general picture of what HR is all about, building a common ground and basic understanding of key HR key themes.

But to allow these bread-and-butter HR activities to come to fruition for your particular business, it takes more. It takes insight into a set of building blocks and context factors that, in their specific combination, determine and color the backbone of your HR strategy, policy, and practices. The look and feel and specific additive flavors, based upon stakeholder preferences and needs, will turn a generic HR model into your company-original HR model, which will carry the power to set up your organization for sustainable success. This is what Section 2 of this book will cover: building blocks, stakeholders, context factors. In this section, I will provide several illustrations from my past experiences in different settings.

In the third and final section, you will discover an effective and efficient method to develop your own company-original HR roadmap for success, a "how-to" guide for jumpstarting your rejuvenated and renewed HR journey, on your way to delivering Standout HR. I will also suggest a number of key performance indicators, or result areas, you might use to evaluate the effectiveness and efficiency of your company original HR. You will also find highly practical information and information on tools you can download.

As a bonus, I will share with you the results of one of my assignments in a healthcare company. For this company I was asked to develop a proposal for a company-original HR model that would have all it takes to become Standout HR. I will share the final report I delivered to my customer, explaining the project phases, key findings and translation into a renewed company-original HR framework that specified four new key HR objectives. This turned their current HR into Standout HR with associated positive impact on the organization's success.

Once you have gone through this book and the available tools, you will understand that the pathway to sustainable success for your business is bringing HR from the outside in, turning your own HR inside out, to deliver Standout HR. Because your business deserves nothing less!

Make sure you do the right thing now for your business, learn how to bring Standout HR into your organization, and harvest the benefits as soon as you dive into this journey! Every dollar spent on anything less than Standout HR is a dollar lost.

GET YOUR
FREE RESOURCE

A very useful and unique tool comes with this book as a free bonus. To make sure you get the most benefit from this book, download the extra tool using the link below:

Standout HR Free bonus

SECTION 1:

GENERIC HR

This section will briefly describe what generic HR looks like. You will see a relatively standard HR model that covers basic HR activities and their elementary themes and domains, topics that are being taught to help students develop a basic understanding of what HR is about. There are many ways to present such an overview, and none is worthier than another.

I will present to you the model I use myself when working with business clients. When I teach students what HR is about, I usually let them develop ideas by thinking and freewheeling about what happens to people from the moment they enter the labor market until the moment they stop working to enjoy retirement.

It comes down to the HR-driven processes an individual will experience, from the moment he or she joins an organization all the way through to exiting that same organization, and possibly multiple times during his or her professional life. It is also often referred to as the employee life cycle. HR is involved in the **inflow** of people, the **through-flow** within the organization, and the **outflow** out of the organization. All these in-, through-, and outflow activities have two **subflows** in common, a set of mainstream activities that link to **compensation and benefits**, and are reinforced by **internal communication** initiatives.

This is called the generic model because it is applicable to every company in every sector in every country; it does not explain how to make a choice between multiple techniques or strategies to perform activities. These choices are strongly dependent upon specifics linked to the company in context and will be covered in the following section.

But first, the basics. Once you have gained an overall understanding of what HR is all about, you will easily bridge to what your business in particular needs in this area. The insights in basic-yet-generic HR will allow you to easily join discussions with your HR leader. You will be recognized and appreciated as a very valuable, thought-provoking sounding board for dialogues on the intersection between your business acumen and HR knowhow.

1.1. Inflow

Inflow stands for all activities related to attracting the people your organization needs, selecting the best ones to join the organization, hiring them, and introducing them to your organization and the team he or she will become part of. It is sometimes also referred to as "talent acquisition."

Prior to engaging in talent acquisition activities, an important decision needs to be made. What sort of collaboration will you set up? There are many different types, and depending upon your specific goals, and a number of other considerations, you might opt for one or another category. Most collaborations can be categorized under one of these:

- Employees
- Interns
- Student workers
- Freelancers
- Contract workers
- Interim workers
- Volunteers

For each of these specific groups, specific legislation is applicable, and all of the below-mentioned activities linked to talent acquisition might slightly differ or require specific nuances. So bear in mind what type of collaboration is most suitable, to next add the applicable legal framework and regulative context in further deploying all activities to attract, select, hire, and board the individuals.

1.1.1. Recruitment

As soon as a single individual selling a product or service finds himself unable or unwilling to continue on his own, the need for some sort of organization becomes imminent. Whenever more than one person gets involved in whatever service or product is being delivered, an organization is born. And when an organization grows, the number of activities and things to take care of not only increases, but also diversifies.

The initiator, or owner of the company, will need to decide how to grow and evolve: Will he or she continue doing it all (from researching and developing, to producing, to marketing, to financing, to quality control, to customer service, to logistics, to after-sales support...), and thus involve others doing exactly the same things, or will this person decide to stick to his talents and delegate other aspects to people who have more competencies in other domains necessary to build a successful business? Henry Mintzberg is considered a guru in organization theory, so I prefer to refer to this research for more info related to how organizations grow, develop, and structure themselves.

As a business leader, you made a set of decisions related to how to organize the work. At certain moments, you needed to make the decision to add staff. Once the decision is made to go out and find additional human resources, you are in the recruiting business. You need to let the outside world know that you are in need of people helping you in your organization and that you have something to offer.

Recruitment has to do with all activities around advertising vacancies and attracting enough people to your organization to provide you with a collection of possible candidates to choose from. It includes promoting yourself and your organization, but also thinking about and making explicit what kind of people you are looking for, what you expect from them, and what you have to offer.

Employer branding becomes an important activity to engage in, specifically when you are fishing in a pond with few fish or lots of fishermen! *Scarcity of talent* and *the war for talent* are widespread expressions that demonstrate the difficulties many organizations experience in attracting viable potential employees. A solid, authentic Employee Value Proposition (EVP) that talks directly to your target audience can be the differentiating factor.

You can decide to do these recruitment activities yourself, or you can call upon recruitment agencies to go out there and find the candidates you are in need of.

1.1.2. Selection

Selecting candidates for your vacancy means verifying to what extent they meet your expectations. Building a detailed and thorough candidate profile is a priority. To do so, you need to be crystal clear about exactly what you need for your organization. You need to be able to list out in detail all activities this person will be responsible for. This translates into specific expertise, experience, abilities, and skill sets: e.g., an accountant needs to be able to perform different tasks than an internal auditor.

However, this is only the starting point. Say you do need an accountant, and you find a number of interested people with either the accounting degree, working experience in an accounting department, or a combination of both. How will you decide who to give the job to? There is a lot more to consider. For instance, the ideal candidate needs to be screened on specific competencies that are linked to the job, the team, and the organization: you might want an autonomous person, someone innovative to explore new ways of organizing all the accounting work, or someone who can grow into a role to make a difference in building a successful team of accountants, or someone who can silently do whatever he is told, applying the existing processes to the letter.

You also need to check to what extent the candidate will fit in, so considering the specificities of your organization in terms of structure, culture, climate, governance, etc., can further refine the profile you are looking for. You might also want to consider specific personality information, given that every person is unique in his or her combination of talents, competencies, skills, aptitudes, and attitudes.

It is also important to examine the candidate's expectations, both in the short- and longer-term, and the extent to which you can answer those. Be aware that when selecting a candidate for the job, you are implicitly agreeing to build a partnership, influencing this person's life.

As you can see, selecting the perfect candidate is far from easy. It is also crucial to be thorough and conscientious , since making the wrong decision is not only very costly for the organization, but can also break one's individual career or professional life. This is why it is strongly recommended to include multiple people and selection specialists in this selection phase, people who have learned how to "read" candidates, and how to objectively look for indications of fit or misfit with the function, team, and organization. Experts can use a combination of techniques, including assessment centers, personality questionnaires, competency-based interviewing using the STAR (**S**ituation, **T**ask, **A**ctivities, **R**esults based questioning) approach, etc. Including multiple people (selection expert, hiring manager, manager +1, peer or future coworker) can help to develop a fuller picture and confidence in a solid and joint decision.

Always remember that your image as an organization is at stake here. So make sure that you treat candidates fairly, that you take this seriously, and that you are ready to justify and explain your choice and your decision with regard to each candidate reviewed.

1.1.3. Contracting your Candidate

Once the candidate that best matches the profile has been identified, and there is a joint agreement of all involved parties to hire this person for the position, you enter the hiring phase.

This is the moment where the "bonding" of the candidate to your organization truly begins. You need to engage in setting up, discussing, and negotiating a contract between both parties, where you take into consideration—besides all legal regulations to adhere to—your company policy and practices (in terms of compensation and benefits package), to give this person a competitive offer that balances the person's expectations with his or her projected added value to your organization, and any other internal and external equity considerations.

1.1.4. Onboarding

The final stage in the inflow or talent acquisition phase is at the same time building the bridge to the next phase (the through-flow or talent development phase). Preparation for onboarding a new collaborator requires a team effort. The new worker needs to provide a number of documents and personal information that the organization needs to complete his or her file, and prepare for payroll processing. Systems accesses and profiles need to be set up; equipment needs to be ordered and prepared; the first couple of days, weeks, and months need to be planned; and the receiving team needs to be informed and involved in the welcoming of the new joiner, among other things.

Besides all logistical preparations, in many companies, the new joiner will receive an initial training schedule with lots of people to meet and an onboarding day where he or she will be immersed into the organization's history, mission, vision and strategy, culture, processes, etc.

Rushing into boarding a new member of the organization is usually not the right thing to do. Spending sufficient time in preparing for his or her arrival, involving multiple people and embracing this event to market and brand your organization through the efforts of others is a huge opportunity to make an impact, good impression, and jumpstart for a great and lasting relationship.

1.2. Through-flow

This second phase in an employee's lifecycle, **through-flow**, is the longest and core part of one's employment in a company: it is the time where the individual develops, grows, performs, contributes to the organization, learns about himself, learns about the organization, learns about the products and services, sees subsequent career paths, engages in future career moves, and finds ways to achieve his aspirations in his professional life. The employee learns about company life, culture, strategy, systems, and processes, but also about dealing with adversity, conflict, etc.

This phase bundles a number of key themes that are all interrelated and refer to development: performance management, assessment of potential, succession planning, and internal mobility.

1.2.1. Development

In every organization, development efforts and investments should form the core of HR focus and budgets. People who do not grow, develop, and learn new skills and capabilities are—in the longer term—losing their value. Even though one might argue that an individual owns his own development, and is the architect of his own career, it is just as much an organization's responsibility to invest in its human resources. In business, people are most likely the differentiating factor, so you'd better make sure to use them to their maximum potential.

The topic of development is immensely broad and massively studied. You will find numerous blog posts, articles, guides, and institutions that will help you to gain full understanding of what development in corporate perspective is all about. In the below section, I merely provide you with a couple of general ideas related to the topic.

Development can be looked at from different perspectives or angles. There is the difference between **personal** and **professional development**, with a very broad grey zone in between. When an individual wants to learn Russian out of curiosity or for touristic purposes, with no links whatsoever to his or her profession, this is an individual need or aspiration that the individual can aim at and work towards. When an individual wants to learn how to be more assertive, this might be a specific business-driven need but with great personal (private) benefits.

In business context, it is always important to have a face-to-face development dialogue between employee and supervisor to truly discuss what kind of development is instrumental for successful performance in the position or in the organization, as opposed to development that is "nice to have" or interesting for future career advancement or personal enrichment.

Within the professionally oriented development, there is the difference between **short-** and **longer-term return on investment**. Developing a technical skill one needs to master to perform basic operations is short-term oriented and probably linked to facilitating the achievement of objectives. When one is aiming to—one day—acquire a leadership position, and the company sees the potential already, it might be good to step up and proactively start to develop, for the longer term, management skills and leadership styles.

You can also make a difference whether the development is aiming to increase one's **individual skills, expertise and capability** or focusing on **team development**. In team development, we are looking at another development dynamic that can and will undoubtedly also impact personal development, but the focus will be on the growth of the team as a team of individuals that mutually reinforce each other and thereby prove that, in team efforts, 1+1 can equal 3.

Another angle through which to look at development concerns the **internal or external focus**. Individuals within the organization can help in developing others; colleagues can go outside to gain specific capabilities that they can then share with their coworkers; or the organization can bring in external knowledge to train or develop a specified group of individual workers. All are ways to invest in a culture of learning from each other, both internally and externally.

In terms of the **sponsor**, the one who will finance trainings, seminars, or other development opportunities, there are also different approaches. It can be fully financed by the organization (both in terms of the actual cost of the training and in terms of the working time spent to attend), or it can be a joint effort (e.g., when the organization pays, but the individual invests his personal private time, or vice versa).

Development opportunities can also be a constituent part of a **company reward strategy**. It is often disregarded or underestimated as a way to provide incentives for colleagues, but it can be a very strong instrument to formally encourage development, sponsoring solid or outstanding performance by dedicating training budgets to those people who step out of the crowd in terms of both efforts and results.

Let's also not forget that there is a tax-friendly aspect related to rewarding people by providing development opportunities instead of salary increases or bonuses. Sending talented and high performing people to highly renowned institutions for training will—on top of the expertise acquired and brought into your organization—uplift the residual value of the coworker in future endeavors and possible career moves within or outside of the organization. The impact on the increased attractiveness of the company to the outside world cannot be neglected, either. This practice can become a talent magnet instrument without having to spend any additional dollars.

Whatever you decide to do in terms of development, make sure that it is consistent, coherent, needs-driven, serving a specific objective, cost effective, and containing a demonstrable and trackable return on investment.

1.2.2. Performance Management

When an individual joins a company, there is a rationale behind it. The organization needs that person, in terms of the conglomerate of skills, competencies, aptitudes, and expertise that he or she brings in, filling a void or answering a specific need that will help the organization to flourish, be successful, and achieve its results.

The best way to achieve those results is to make sure that the person knows exactly what is expected, and what needs to be realized. The person can only be successful if he knows what he is up against and what success in his specific situation and position looks like. Joint **goal setting**, or mutually agreeing upon what needs to be achieved, is an important priority between the organization and the new employee.

Enabling the person to achieve the results is a second phase. This is where **coaching and development** step in. It is crucial to understand what it takes to become a good performer, and to make sure the person has the necessary skills, tools and support to be successful. Thinking through the specific needs to be able to realize the set objectives should result in a solid development plan, one of the key enablers for an individual's success and continued growth.

Periodic review of where the colleague is on the journey to success and to the achievement of goals is another important activity. This is the time to look back at the road already walked, the progress made towards the end results. It is the time to evaluate whether or not one is on the right track to success. This is usually called a performance review. If both colleague and manager agree that everything is on track, there is an opportunity for reinforcement of mutual trust. It also validates that the employee is successfully performant, which is crucial for keeping up the pace and quality of achievement. If not, redirection might be needed and additional measures and initiatives may need to be envisaged, so that one gets back on track and failure is avoided. Performance improvement plans can become a useful instrument in these situations of suboptimal performance.

In many companies there is a classic one-year performance cycle that each person goes through, beginning with goal setting, moving through to development planning, then an intermediate or mid-year review, and ending with a year-end assessment of performance against set goals and standards. Current research and thinking goes against this type of "forced" cycle with its imposed moments. It proposes to have these performance dialogues in a more informal and continued way, and opens the door to more organic and constant feedback to constantly monitor and guide performance and progress.

Some companies have introduced—in addition to this individual objectives-setting and performance management approach—a more team-oriented or collective flavor to performance management.

Irrespective of what your organization chooses, it is crucial that every individual clearly understands how he or she is contributing to the overall success of the team, department, and organization. This increases the sense of belonging and the perception of being a substantial part of the chain of success. It will indirectly increase engagement, productivity, and retention.

1.2.3. Identification of Potential – Talent Reviews

More and more companies are engaging in what is usually called a **talent review**. The top talents are being identified, through a roll-up approach, starting at the lowest level and moving all the way up to the C-suite, so that top management gains a good idea of the number of talented people (defined as high performers, high potentials, or a combination of both), the spread throughout the organization, and the specific expertise the company has in-house.

What is crucial here is that the discussion needs to be focused on talents, and on potential, not necessarily or exclusively on performance. Top performers need to be rewarded, recognized, and reinforced to continue to perform at the top level, but those who are not yet there but have shown sparks of talent need to be brought to the surface at the earliest possible stage.

These reviews help to make the talent agenda visible throughout the organization, and can be the starting point for specific additional development investments toward high potentials to steer and direct their further development.

It can also be a starting point to engage in development centers for people who are being identified as high potentials, or talents, that are very promising but not yet at their maximum performance level. For this category of people, it is often worthwhile to invest in development centers. During such a development center (often external to the organization), a deep dive into specific competencies is set up so that a relatively objective measurement can be done. This has proven helpful to focus and direct development actions to bring the potential to maximum fruition by orchestrating specific exposures through sought-out experiences, projects, coaching, executive mentoring, etc.

Since the starting point in this context is the individual and his or her talents and potential, a talent review is applicable. The other side of the coin is that the organization takes a look at what talents are available to safeguard or build the organization's future. In this exercise, **succession planning** is the primary focus.

1.2.4. Succession Planning

When we are taking the perspective of the organization, it is of crucial importance that the key positions are at all times properly filled, and that there are contingency plans available for when employees move. People moving out of a critical position can be planned and prepared for, specifically when this is part of the talent review results. However, it can also happen that a critical position holder leaves the organization unexpectedly.

Whether or not it is company-intentional, when a critical position holder vacates there needs to be a successor within a relatively short period of time. Indeed, if a critical position can withstand vacancy for multiple months, without having any negative business risk or impact, you might wonder whether the position deserves to be labeled "critical."

Succession planning—initially focusing on the business-critical and top management positions—is the process of reviewing with top management the succession urgency (e.g., immediate, 6 months, 1 year, longer). Potential candidates are then discussed who can be prepared or are ready to step in and succeed the current incumbent. This is the perfect exercise to build harmony between the talent review on the one hand, where high potentials have been identified and potential tracks, development opportunities, and experiences have been discussed, and succession planning on the other hand.

The individual's aspiration and potential can be matched to a succession need, and vice versa. In the affirmative scenario, a candidate can be prepared in an adequate and in a highly focused way to succeed his predecessor. Alternatively, this kind of balance exercise might highlight that there are succession gaps that need to be acted upon by potential external recruiting or intensified internal development.

Once people start moving, the domino effect occurs all throughout the organization, creating some new dynamics that can boost development, engagement, innovation, and growth.

1.2.5. Internal Mobility

Internal mobility refers to all the position changes that employees enact. In most organizations, whenever there is a new vacancy (due to a person leaving the company, moving to another role, headcount increase, organizational changes, etc.), this opportunity is usually initially opened for internal applications, making maximum use of available talent and ambitions or career aspirations.

Employees can take the initiative to apply to a vacancy within the organization, but they can also be stimulated by management to take up some new role. It might be the right next step in terms of their career, an intermediate action towards their end goal. As a result of the succession planning exercise, people might be appointed to a specific new position, creating a vacancy in their previous position. Employees leaving the company, voluntarily or intentionally, can also generate vacancies to open up for internal and external applications.

Employees can move around in all possible directions, upon their own initiative or following the company's proposals. These moves entail promotions, demotions, and lateral moves, among others. All of this movement, as long as it is controlled and not chaos-inducive, creates the kind of dynamics an organization needs to continue evolving.

Whenever a person starts in a new position or team or department, you will often see that the new incumbent offers innovative ways of looking at things that were always there, generating innovative approaches, inducing change and reflection. This is a positive vibe to encourage and support, just as from time to time, it can happen that an employee's immediate future lies outside of an organization. There is absolutely nothing wrong with that; it can even happen, and one should embrace this occasion, that an ex-employee returns later on, with refreshed ideas, and a partly common or shared history.

1.3. Outflow

Outflow refers to all activities linked to ending employment. There are a multitude of circumstances under which employees leave the organization. We will briefly highlight some potential situations and what is important to consider when these happen.

Although largely underestimated and heavily neglected in many cases, effective and solid knowledge management should be your primary concern, whenever employment within the position comes to an end. Finally, mechanisms like in- and outplacement are important image builders, as are a number of alternatives for effective workforce management.

1.3.1. Ending Employment

Working with employees means working within the legal framework of a professional relationship bound by legal restrictions, regulations that differ from country to country, across different states, and depending upon the specific type of contract that was agreed upon. Both parties have rights and obligations that reside in a mutually signed agreement. The most important advice is to ensure that you have a specialist supporting you all the way through the process, from setting up an employment relationship and contract, through modifying, altering or adding attachments, to ending it. Dollars spent on lawsuits or even simple discussions or conflict resolution are dollars better spent on other topics.

What is important to note is that both parties have similar rights in terms of ending or breaching an employment contract. As a good employer, make sure that you help your employee to understand and respect those rights whenever he or she takes the initiative to end employment. I recall numerous cases of employees resigning without even being aware of longer-term consequences to their personal situations. Be a good employer for your company and also for those who are leaving; you never know what the future might bring!

There are multiple reasons to end employment. From the organization's perspective, these are the most frequently used reasons:

- Low or underperformance of the employee
- Poor match between company culture and employee attitude and behavior
- Ending contract of defined or limited duration, usually with end date explicitly agreed upon up-front
- Business reasons linked to decreases in workload, products being put out of the market, economic downfall
- Headcount reduction as a means to cut down on overall business costs
- Mutual termination agreement between employer and employee because of conflicting interests, expectations, etc.
- Employee misdemeanors, leading to a breach of internal policy and regulations within the organization
- Employees hurting the organization's image because of external misdemeanors or criminal convictions

Make sure to make the decision to end a collaboration with proper care, after sufficient consideration and consultation of all people involved. Equally important is how you go about actually doing this. Assuming you have all legal constraints covered, make sure to stand up as an ethical, deontological, human, professional employer, preparing the situation carefully, taking all the time needed to communicate and follow up on all subsequent actions. Make sure the concerned employee is well cared for, understands the reason underlying this decision, the impact, and any future obligations. Involve his or her team members if appropriate, and make sure to allow sufficient time for all involved to "digest" the news, cope with it, and put it in the correct perspective.

Always remember that these are life-changing events, both for the impacted employee, and also for his immediate private and professional social environment. The way you are handling this will be observed, will be remembered, and will mark you both as an employer and as a person. It is important to be aware of the impact around the specific situation, and also far beyond that. Your image is at stake regarding how you will be positioned in the labor market, and how you will survive in comparison with your business competition. Ending employment thus might generate indirect effects that can last for ages when you are recruiting again or trying to "buy in" people from competitive companies, etc.

Since there are two parties in a collaboration agreement, the employee (or contract worker, freelancer, temp, student, intern, etc.), can also decide to breach or end the agreement, end employment, and hand in a resignation. Such a decision tends to give rise to very diverse reactions depending upon the situation, the level of surprise, and the perception of the person's talents.

Irrespective of any feelings of regret, anger, disappointment, loss, frustration, or non-comprehension, the first thing to do is to sit down and listen. If nothing else, please make sure you understand the person's rationale, and specifically what lies beyond his initial arguments and explanation. There are tools out there (exit interviews or surveys) that can help you ask the best questions to generate the information you need for your own learning. Analyzing reasons why specific categories of staff leave might be highly valuable for future action planning and specific retention initiatives.

1.3.2. Knowledge Management

For many of you reading this book, this section on **knowledge management** probably comes as a surprise. Many organizations do not adequately develop systems, processes, or tools to effectively manage their knowledge. Can you imagine the risk of people leaving the organization if the knowledge about how they were contributing to your business only resides in their heads? In many cases, this is not fiction!

Unfortunately, knowledge management is often restricted to the development of databases, exclusively from an IT perspective, with the hope that knowledge accumulates there and is used optimally. The initial definition of knowledge management was cited as follows: *"Knowledge management is the process of capturing, distributing, and effectively using knowledge"* (Davenport, 1994). Later, the Gartner Group created another definition, which has become the one most frequently cited: *"Knowledge management is a discipline that promotes an integrated approach to identifying, capturing, evaluating, retrieving, and sharing all of an enterprise's information assets. These assets may include databases, documents, policies, procedures, and previously un-captured expertise and experience in individual workers"* (Duhon, 1998). It is specifically this last addition of "un-captured expertise and experience in individual workers" that is important in our context.

If your business means the world to you, and thrives on knowledge, expertise, capability, and experience, take sufficient precautions and install a process to capture people's knowledge and *savoir faire* prior to them leaving. If there is one thing you should invest in, it is making sure that your staff's knowledge gets consolidated within your organization. If this is not the case, you become extremely vulnerable and dependent upon the most volatile element in your business model: your people. This can be your ultimate weakness, or it could become your ultimate force, depending upon how you deal with it.

Once you are fully convinced of the need to have something like a knowledge management practice in place, make sure you extend it to every bit of knowledge that is developed throughout the life cycle of your product, your equipment, your team, and your individual colleagues, so that, when it comes to someone ending employment, all you need to do is verify if everything is well captured and in shape for handing over to the organization. This will put you in much better shape to deal with the uncertainty of the length of the relationship with your staff and their "brains."

Your need for effective knowledge management in case of resignations or dismissals can be properly handled if you agree to this up front and make people truly understand that this is part of "the deal of working here." In case of leaving one's position, whether it is to move to another position within the organization, to move to a new role or project within the current function, or to leave the department or even organization entirely, you need to spend time, effort, and resources to provide for a full handover of internalized knowledge into a system, tool, or colleague. There are many ways to go about this. All you need to do is involve someone who can help you in setting this up. There are many tools, resources and specialists out there, to prevent the risk of losing what is in fact yours to begin with!

1.3.3. Workforce Management

There are numerous books on **workforce management**, so I do not have the audacity to even try and summarize this subject. I do want to mention the topic because in the context of letting people go or losing people, it might be helpful to think about the optimal way to manage your workforce and more specifically some non-conventional ways to consider dealing with intentional or unplanned changes in workforce needs.

Whenever your organization is confronted with a need to reduce the workforce, due to a period of slowed growth, economic downturn, a failed product launch, high labour costs that are not absorbed by sufficient revenue, etc., there are multiple ways to deal with this. As a good business leader, you need to sit down with your management team to gain in-depth insight into the specifics of the situation, the urgency to mitigate, and all possible options to deal with this setback.

If some of your valued employees need to leave the organization, it might be a good option to consider investing in outplacement services. Outplacement services are usually provided by external and specialised firms that coach the impacted people in their quest for a new job. These consultants will help the impacted employees through their grief and mourning period, and will guide them to reflect upon themselves and to redirect their lives toward new horizons, via specific coaching, skills building, action planning, and effective job-hunting.

In some circumstances and countries, this might be a legal and mandatory action; in others, not, but nevertheless, helping people find a new future when you no longer are able to provide this for them is not only a very human thing to do, it is also a lucrative action. Think about what this would mean for those impacted;they will very much respect you for doing this. But also think about the remaining employees, and their perception of what is happening: they will highly appreciate the efforts you are making to help their co-workers and will think very highly of you, which will undoubtedly increase their engagement and willingness to do whatever it takes to help you and the organization. They will use this company gesture to truly act as ambassadors toward the outside world, promoting your company to customers, competitors, and future co-workers.

In-management is also a concept that you could consider applying. With in-management, you take the lead in finding other assignments or jobs for your people within other parts of your company, or outside of your company. This can be a worthwhile strategy, when you consider that in the longer-term, you might need these people back. You can"send them out" to help other companies (within or outside of the same market or within your own network), or to develop new skills.

Another mechanism to control or manage your workforce is to diversify the categories of people you work with: e.g., temps, volunteers, freelancers, employees, interns, consultants, or contract employees. They all differ in terms of what they can bring to your company, what they typically cost you, what type of flexibility they give you in using them, etc.

1.4. Subflow

All activities and themes mentioned in the sections on inflow, through-, and outflow have a common denominator. They all link to, cannot do without, and greatly influence two other sets of **subflow** activities: **compensation and benefits** on the one hand and **internal communication** on the other hand. We will briefly touch upon both in this section. The aim is to give you a very clear idea of the reasons why these activities are or should be part of any generic HR model. As you surely know, these topics are so broad and deep that we could fill a whole library with information.

1.4.1. Compensation and Benefits

The very foundation of any formal and usually written relationship between an individual and an organization is that, against certain services rendered, an agreed-upon pay or reimbursement of some kind takes place. Performing labour initiates the right to get paid. Receiving some kind of gratification for what you offer to a third party is the principle that makes the world turn around. However, in organizational context it can become highly complex, since there are many parties involved, there is a whole system of taxation and declaration behind it, and it usually covers a number of derived benefits that make life easier in our society. But nothing is for free, so every benefit offered comes with a price, and a price paid needs to be funded from someplace else.

There are many different aspects in rewarding your people for their work. Times are long gone when people were satisfied to receive their paycheck at the end of the month. There are so many ways of "paying" people that a vast number of experts have been focusing on differentiating compensation elements into compensation practices, using lots of research and studies to develop the best way to pay, reward, and treat your workforce.

In defining your own internal compensation and benefits policy, there are multiple elements to consider:

- Internal equity should be one of your key design criteria, without which all the efforts spent to develop a highly competitive and motivational yet economic system will go down the drain. If internal equity is impacted, you will by default induce conflict. Internal equity does not mean "the same for everyone"; on the contrary, there needs to be differentiation, but similar and transparent rules and an objective application to justify and even necessitate differences.

- External equity makes business life in the current economy liveable. You would not do justice to the market economy if you pay people extravagantly more or less than your competitors. Where you can differentiate is in the way you develop a well-balanced basket of compensation elements, where the totality will stand out, reflecting your own philosophy and vision and also appealing most to those talents you are looking for.

- Internal budgets will of course also be one of the driving forces for developing your compensation and benefits policies. Some benefits might be "cheaper" in the eyes of your people, or generating less direct cash or income but generating a bigger remuneration impact than other types of rewards (e.g., deferred bonus payments as part of pension schemes, trainings that provide specific valuable certification, etc.). These effective remuneration instruments might be less applauded by your target audience. Proper positioning, branding, and marketing are supporting factors in these situations. A balanced budget with sufficient buffer for the unexpected, and with some extra cans to pour from whenever differential rewarding becomes necessary, requires divestiture, proper analysis, forecasting, and constant monitoring.

STANDOUT HR • 42

- The degree of complexity in administering and managing personnel pay and personnel administration is another factor to consider. You might be very keen on working with both fixed and variable pay, with a cafeteria plan full of all types of reward elements (from company cars, to vacation days, to ICT, to insurances, to stock options). But if your organization is not mature, capable, or big enough to manage, administer, and monitor this, it will lead to chaos, frustration, and dissatisfaction and it might be better to opt for a plain, simple, equitable, and transparent package. Remember that in the pyramid of HR services, you want most of your HR resources helping you to implement your business strategy. If you need half an army to run all transactional payroll related activities, you will lose out on HR providing business value-adding contributions.

- Finally, do not forget that rewarding people has a recognition element as well. Recognizing contributions, however plain or extraordinary they may be, is paramount in binding your workforce to you, motivating them to show up every day and make your business dream come true. Having them spontaneously go the extra mile or provide the effort your business deserves is what will make you prosper. It is important to ensure your policy incorporates and reflects this more than anything else.

1.4.2. Internal Communication

Working in HR implies working with and for people. Communication is not only the vehicle, but should be at the core of what HR does, needs, and uses. Unfortunately, this is where many HR departments (and organizations, to make a generalization) run short. Few HR departments have an internal communications team, expert, or role dedicated to ensure that whatever HR does, provides, or supports is effectively relayed to those who need to know, be involved, and make use of it.

When you review everything we have touched upon so far, how much more powerful would it all be if we—right from the start—included an effective communication plan.

- Posting a vacancy to the internal and external market, is an act of communication, or should in essence be one. Yet, we focus more on the wording than on the message, more on the channel than on the positioning, more on the generation of hits than on the branding.
- Whenever we have people developing themselves so they can live up to the challenge of a specific business project, do we communicate about this?
- How often do we miss out on opportunities simply because we do not think proactively about the communication part, or we are so busy that, last minute, we realize, "Oh yeah, we should have our CEO send out an email to welcome Brad, who started this morning, so that people know what he's here for and can make him feel welcome."
- When we have to let someone go, for whatever reason, how well do we prepare and cascade proper messages to all target audiences? And to what extent have we prepared the ones in charge of this particular communication so they feel comfortable enough to convey these messages?

I can go on and on and on about every single activity HR is involved in that entails a communication aspect. We all know how important it is, yet, we tend to make a mess of it time after time after time. I cannot stress enough that internal communication is crucial and critical; it is the glue that can build a strong, focused work force, a team of people that have confidence in their leaders and in those who take care of them. Your people can be your ambassadors to the outside world, creating a huge impact.

So make sure to spend enough time, energy, resources, and funds to dialogue, consult, and communicate with your people. This, and only this, can build your employer reputation and have significant effects on employer branding, on internal and external attractiveness, on talent retention, and on business growth and prosperity, even in adverse times.

1.5. The generic HR Model Overview

Bringing it all together, the generic and basic HR model, covering basic core HR activities, can be visualized as in the below overview. Luckily, there are many more activities HR engages in, activities that will feed or paint the way this basic model comes alive. More about this in the following section.

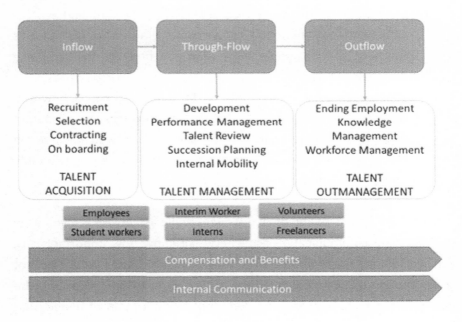

SECTION 2:

COMPANY-ORIGINAL HR

I n this section we will describe what elements you need to take into consideration when developing your own HR. Company-original HR will evolve when you adapt the general HR model by integrating three distinct sets of elements into your company-original set up: **internal building blocks, external factors, and your stakeholders**.

These three sets of factors will determine the DNA of your HR model. They are factors that will enable or facilitate the way your HR strategy takes form, the accents to put in place, and the choices to make in implementing specific HR programs. The totality and company-specific combination of these factors will bring your own HR to life, and it will differentiate the way you do HR from another organization's method. It will shape, define, and color your HR strategy. It will create interdependencies and mutual reinforcements of separate HR practices.

Setting up HR through these lenses (building blocks, external elements, and stakeholders) will lead to one integrated, thought-through, business foundational approach. It will bring that company-specific flavor that your business needs to introduce Standout HR.

Standout HR, which breathes your organization's DNA, will lay the groundwork for results for your organization that go beyond the classic (generic) HR impact, and will set your organization at top performance in terms of change-aptitude and agility, organizational development, engagement, employability, and well-being. It is these characteristics, that, driven by company-original HR, will set your organization apart from all others.

2.1. Internal building Blocks

HR is not a profession that you perform in isolation. HR is a discipline that develops a set of activities designed to help the organization flourish. The specificities and particularities of the organization will determine how HR will align its activities with the organization's characteristics.

We will describe a number of **building blocks** that have proven to be of crucial importance in customizing the generic HR model. This is most definitely not an exhaustive list, but it is what I have found helpful to take into account. They are elements that will determine what nuances to bring into company-original HR. Building blocks are activities one needs to engage in prior to rolling out core HR. These building blocks form the foundation, the cement, to build your HR upon.

In this context, I often refer to McKinsey's 7S framework. This framework was developed as a tool to structure an internal organizational analysis, and I find it helpful to determine what to focus on in terms of organizational change. The 7S model was developed and published by Thomas Peters and Robert Waterman (*In Search of Excellence*, 1982), Richard Pascale, and Anthony Athos, all of whom were working at the consultancy house McKinsey at the time. It has become one of the most widespread, valuable, and commonly used frameworks to gain insight in the way an organization is set up, develops and gains success. "7S" refers to the seven identified 7 internal factors that link together and influence each other: **Strategy, Structure, and Systems** on the one hand, the so-called "hard factors," and **Staff, Style, Shared beliefs, and Skills** on the other hand, the "soft factors."

When looking at how to align your HR (referred to in the 7S model as "Staff") with the rest of your company's key identifiers, it is important to bring to the surface what will determine, or at least influence, your HR strategy. Inspired by this model, I usually look at and describe key company-specific insights linked to **strategy, structure, and culture**. Other elements I take into consideration when gaining a first understanding of the organization's key characteristics include its **history, scale, maturity,**

and governance. Finally, and partly based upon the analysis of the above-mentioned perspectives, prior to diving into core HR it is important to define your **function/role structure** and the focus on **competencies and/or talents**.

2.1.1. History, Scale, Maturity, and Governance

An organization's **history** can be a blessing or a curse. In any case, ignoring it is setting up your HR strategy for failure. When looking back at your organization's history, try to bundle it in a couple of key milestones that have defined what your company currently looks like. Then, identify what decisions took place to achieve those milestones and what could have been alternative options that were not chosen. The reasons why certain options were not chosen can provide you important background information. The history an organization has built up can also shed some light on its **internal maturity**, and the way it deals with numerous intentional or unexpected situations. Having dealt with multiple new product launches, for example, will have a positive impact on the maturity in preparing for a new launch, as compared to a company's very first time doing such a thing.

It goes without saying that the current **size of your organization** is another important identifier that will impact the way you do business and thus, the way you look at HR. When you are in the startup phase of your business, lots of attention will be given to recruitment and employer branding. However, it might be useful to extend that to developing the people you bring on board at the same speed as you want your company to develop. At the early stages in your company growth, you as business leader will still have a lot to learn and to discover, so your focus should be on development, both self-development as well as development of your business. Deciding how you will inject growth in your company will massively impact your HR strategy.

Think about the differences between organic growth and growth through mergers and acquisitions. In the organic growth scenario, you will be at the steering wheel, with decisive power in the kind of people you board, the products and services you develop, and the culture you breed. Growth will happen almost unknowingly, smoothly, not necessarily slowly, but at least pretty gradually.

Growth by acquisition is much more disruptive, determining your future outlook by bringing in business, practices, habits, and people that potentially conflict with your past and alter your culture, your outlook, your business strategy, and your positioning in your market. You should not underestimate the effect of taking over a company, from the perspective of both the one being taken over, and your own original organization. This kind of organizational growth and change will require totally different HR skills and themes than in organic growth situations.

When an organization grows, the need for **governance** will also grow. Governance can become a very limiting canvas in some situations, whereas in others, it can be your life vest. Understanding the situation you are in, and the way governance is impacting your business and is perceived by your different stakeholders, is again important information to help align your HR strategy to your company and customize it to achieve maximal fit. These reflections will colour your HR choices and help you in developing your own standout HR.

2.1.2. Strategy, Structure, and Culture

As a business leader, you are probably better positioned than myself or any HR leader to discuss your own **strategy, structure, and culture**. These three concepts form the foundation of your organization.

Most business leaders have affinity with the **strategy** of their company, which is logical, as you are the one leading your business to success, you are the one with the vision of the future, you are driving your company down the road to success. What is important, and often neglected, is that your HR leader needs to be very much in line with your thinking, grasping at least some of your passion for it. Your HR leader needs to understand what it is you are trying to accomplish, where you want to go, and how you plan to get there, so that HR initiatives can support you in this endeavor and help identify and pave the best road to your goals. In a number of cases, HR is doomed to fail simply because the "off-the-shelf-"solution does not match your strategy.

Illustration: Fast and Furious Recruiting!

In the early nineties, I was given the opportunity to join a company in the telecom industry, as brand new (and first-time) HR manager. The company was a start-up in my country. I was the ninth person to join the team. Since we were looking at massive growth, I engaged a couple of recruitment agencies to help me brand the company to attract the right staff. When I was at the point of publishing vacancies, the first thing I did was develop an extensive job description template questionnaire, with pages and pages for the leaders to define job description information, including context, long-term perspectives, job specifications, requirements, etc. I wanted to do it "the right way." My business leaders were not really thrilled— to say the least—and sent the incomplete template back to me.

I needed a different approach, one that was much more in line with company strategy at that time: growing fast, making quick decisions, taking calculated risks, and evolving. So I needed to go ahead with some very elementary, rough, basic information about the jobs, focusing on what kind of people with the right background we were looking for. I then brought hundreds of candidates together in a big company recruitment event and had my business leaders present the company, their challenges, and their passion. They talked about all available opportunities and interacted with the candidates to check for fit. I had many of these conversation recorded.

It was only later, when a number of people had joined, that I took the time to jointly develop with the new employees their job descriptions and yearly objectives, and this was finally validated by the business leaders.

In HR textbooks, this was definitely not the way to go about things, but in adhering to the strategy (fast, dynamic, calculated into the market), I learned a better way of coming to similar results, one that was accepted by the business and even contributed to it by making more explicit what was expected from those new employees in those new positions. Above all, I learned a great deal more by listening to their speeches than I could have by reading their input in the forms I used!

Business leaders usually do not spend a lot of time reflecting on how to build an effective **organizational structure**. In the latest thinking about structure, there are voices raised about limiting structure, to allow for networking to develop organically and spontaneously. Joint engagement on reaching the objectives and delivering on the promised outcomes should be sufficient. I can adhere to this, in certain contexts, where companies are still "manageable" this way, and history, or scope and magnitude, do not get in the way. When a company grows, whether it is in staff, in products, in volume, in reach, in customer differentiation, or in geographical spread, at some point, minimal structure will be necessary.

As a business leader, you should always question your organizational structure as soon as you see that people start hiding behind it, when processes are slowing down, and when people do not seem to know who to ask or where to go for specific information or outcomes.

Structures highly link to **hierarchical levels**. The flatter an organization can be, the more transparent and dynamic it will operate. Hierarchies usually add control, governance, and clearances to move forward or to step back. Employees, on the other hand, tend to take advantage of their manager to make the decisions for them, or even to think in their place. Management often derails into rendering people incapable or "handcuffed." In psychology workbooks, there is a concept known as "learned helplessness," a true problem that is hiding behind the corner when more and more layers are added to your business structure. It is important to verify that there are always good reasons to install a certain structure, or to add a level of authority, decision making, or management. You risk losing the momentum and free minds of your most talented people when they do not feel "personally touched" by what they are doing day after day.

A structure can be suffocating to some, but a lack of it can be overwhelming and frightening to others, hence the importance of having HR truly understand what works best in your specific situation and to make that happen with the people you are counting on. This is why it is an essential building block to include in your company-original, Standout HR.

Finally, **culture** is the biggest factor in this trio that impacts how to run HR. Culture is the externalization of internal shared values and beliefs that define a company and differentiate it from its competitors. It is the most intangible, yet at the same time most definitive, factor that is seen, felt, expressed, and experienced when looking at the DNA of an organization.

Illustration: Interaction Between Structure and Culture ("CEO, I have a problem")

When I was working as an HR Business Partner in the HR team of a pharm company, I had the privilege of participating occasionally with the executive management team, where the CEO and his direct reports discussed business every two weeks. One of the CEO's direct reports was the Director of Hospital Care, and he was one of my own internal clients at that time. This person, let's call him Vincent, had joined the company through a merger less than a year ago. Vincent was a seasoned leader, with high expertise in his area, and was very much appreciated and thought highly of within the company. He was very respectful to his peers and spoke highly of his manager, the CEO.

This CEO had joined the company just a couple of months prior, was a decade younger, and was an expat with high potential who was extremely intelligent, highly reserved, composed, calm, and patient. When you were presenting something during a meeting where he was present, he hardly intervened, but you could feel and see that in his thinking he was miles ahead of your own story. This was at times intimidating, but on the other hand, it was very encouraging to see this much dedicated thinking and attention.

Vincent highly respected him and tended to take on the position of subordinate. Whenever he brought a topic to the table, he started with "Sir, we have a problem." This was his approach in his previous company where structure, hierarchy, and utter respect for your superiors was prevailing. It was common practice to signal potential issues and ask for immediate decisions and solutions by your manager. That was his role at the time.

Well, not in this setting. Vincent did bring up a couple of issues this way, but the new CEO did not buy it, on the contrary, he politely asked him to go back and reassess the situation. I literally saw Vincent struggling with this—it was clear he felt smaller and smaller, and was reluctant to speak up. Finally, the CEO said the following: "Vincent, you do not have a problem. You have an opportunity. Please go back to your team, and clarify this opportunity and all possible options it generates, then come back with your preferred option to discuss with this management team."

You cannot imagine how powerful this message was. Vincent took it back to his own team, used the same approach with his team and empowered them to develop solutions for and with him. This was a major breakthrough in the formal management of this department. And whenever Vincent asked for an intervention or raised a topic at the management team, he started with, "Dear colleagues, we came across a huge opportunity, let me share the details with you."

2.1.3. Function Structure and Competencies Versus Talents

Functions have always been the single smallest unit of an organization. Every basic activity within core and generic HR also uses the function, position, or job description as a starting point. When you express the need to increase sales by adding people to your workforce, your HR partner will first and foremost ask you what specific function you have in mind: account executive, account manager, sales representative, junior outbound collaborator, presales consultant, sales manager, etc. Based upon your response, a job description will be developed, updated, or used to draft a vacancy text to publish, and to get the recruitment and talent acquisition up and running.

Similarly, your HR partner will use the function and additional requested requirements, such as educational credentials and experience level, to calculate the headcount cost of hiring this future employee (and hopefully HR will partner with Finance regarding budgetary resources and financial forecasts). Base salary benchmarks and seniority level for this particular headcount will be determined based upon the function you requested. Additional benefits linked to this position (e.g., company car, cell phone, variable pay), are derived from your compensation and benefits policy. Based upon the specifics of the function, a preliminary training plan can start being developed.

Using only functions or positions, however, can be a suffocating and limiting structural element. Depending upon your company genetics, it might be a good approach. On the other hand, working with **roles** within a company setup or within a team or project can be an alternative approach. This will allow for much more freedom and flexibility in everything that follows in terms of hiring, training, monitoring, coaching, etc. Working with roles as opposed to functions is of course the other end of what could be seen as a continuum.

In my personal experience, I have always felt the need and added value of providing basic, relatively generic, not-too-detailed function information, complemented with a lot of role- and project-related information. Functions and their interrelations provide framework, context, structure, and security. Roles provide freedom, flexibility, margin, and insecurity. The best of both worlds might in some cases be the best approach. Whichever you decide, this is where the development of company-original, Standout HR steps in.

What is important to ensure is that, as soon as a strategic decision is made in this respect, all preparatory work that is a consequence of this choice is being executed as quickly as possible. Defining your function/role structure provides strategically founded but elementary info that is needed to get your core HR activities up and running. So if you decide, for example, to work with generic functions added with role and project information for an account manager position, set time and resources aside to develop these "extended function descriptions" so that both HR and the business can use these documents, templates, and information for their own core activities. When, at a certain moment in time, the decision is made to hire another account manager, both the hiring manager and HR can jumpstart by using the available company-original account manager function and role description to get the ball rolling.

Another important strategic discussion to have is linked to the use of **competencies and/or talents**. Competency-based thinking relates to the way organizations look at functions needed to have organizational success, and what an individual needs to be able to do to be successful in this function. It is an organization-determined and "top down" approach.

For every function, there is a definition of what it takes to be able to perform the activities that lead to a successful execution: capabilities, skills, knowledge, or to label it with an all-encompassing term, competencies. There are multiple definitions for this concept. At the University of Nebraska-Lincoln, the following definition is used: *Competency: The combination of observable and measurable knowledge, skills, abilities, and personal attributes that contribute to enhanced employee performance and ultimately result in organizational success. (The definition of competencies and their utilization at NU, https://www.unl.edu)*

Many companies have invested in developing and using a company-specific competency dictionary, describing those core or key competencies that are linked to successful performance in a job. For each of those competencies, different levels of competency mastery are described, with a number of behavioral indicators to allow for objective measurements. Competency assessments are then used to evaluate to what extent an individual is competent for the job and what gaps are still imminent and need to be closed. This is in essence a gap-oriented approach: the company/function needs an identified level of competency, the individual only possesses or demonstrates x% of it, and needs to live up to the standards by further training, development, or coaching. In any case, the standard set out by the organization is the base measure; one needs to live up to these expectations to be successful in the assigned function.

Another approach is the strengths-based one. This reflects rather the opposite thinking, focusing on the individual and his or her strengths. This means more than "something one is good at," and includes the elements of losing track of time while doing it (being "in the flow"), experiencing excitement thinking about it or anticipating getting started, and feeling energized when it's completed. Marcus Buckingham and Donald Clifton (*Now, Discover Your Strengths, 2001*) developed this framework based upon analyzing the results of a Gallup study of two million people. Luk Dewulf (*Ik Kies Voor Mijn Talent*, 2009) developed a similar framework that is also widely used in corporate contexts.

This strengths-based approach takes the individual's talents and key added value as a starting point and focuses on creating the best possible environment to let these talents float, grow and develop, thereby contributing to the company's success. An individual in a specific function will then flourish, but will also need help executing activities that are energetically draining because they are not part of the talent pallet of this person. Job crafting, job sharing, and other techniques can then be used to achieve the maximum fit between individual's aspirations and contributions and the organization's needs.

Deciding what kind of framework your organization will benefit from the most, or best fits with the company's DNA, can make huge differences in how to approach specific core HR activities. Company-original HR will come in and make the differential impact.

Illustration: Performance Reviews Revisited

While working at a social profit organization, we were building HR from scratch. The first thing we needed to do was develop a pay structure based upon a functional structure. We therefore launched a project to develop function descriptions to enable us to differentiate and link them to a basic salary structure. It took us multiple months to complete the groundwork and reach an agreement with our social partners, so we were very keen to take it a step further and use the newly developed job descriptions to introduce goal setting and performance review discussions.

Although the benefits of this new development were apparent to all employees and to management—developing clarity in expectations and structured discussions on goal setting and achievement—our social partners were anxious that we would use this approach to "justify dismissals." It clearly showed that the time was not right, and one of our key stakeholders was not buying in to this.

So after some reflection, we developed a more strengths-based approach to allow discussions about expectations to take place. We worked from the perspective of the individual function holder and with the focus on how the organization could maximally contribute to the well-being of its people while enabling them to demonstrate their talents and compensate for activities that were not fully covered.

This was a brand new way of looking at things, and therefore we needed to initially prepare management to understand and buy in to the benefits of this approach. Additionally, we needed to invest in building capability within the management and supervisors to enable them to actually have these conversations with their team members. And with the framework itself being brand new to the people, we needed to develop this prior to applying it in HR processes.

So we decided to take a step back from introducing formal performance reviews so that we could invest in introducing the concept of strengths-based coaching, prior to developing a process that would eventually lead to performance reviews.

2.2. External Factors

HR is not a profession that is performed in a vacuum. HR is a discipline that is highly dependent upon and driven by its context. It is in essence about working with people in organizations that form a constituent part of society. The way to deal with "human aspects" in organizational life is also very much subject to a set of formal legislative regulations. Your company's footprint, both in terms of geography, products, and services, as well as demography, will determine the specific characteristics of the external market that your company-original HR will have to take into consideration.

I will briefly highlight some elements to consider, knowing that this is not an exhaustive overview. Again, these reflections will need to take place prior to and during the development of a company-original HR. If not, you'll get stuck with a generic HR model, which might satisfy your basic HR needs but will not suffice to make the mpact you are expecting to bring the success you are aiming for.

2.2.1. Society, Economics, and Politics

As an organization, you are building society and you have an impact on the society you are part of. On the other hand, whatever society dictates, whatever is "hot in town," can generate an impact on or influence what happens in your organization. Given the topic of this book – standout HR – I will limit my views on societal impact to the HR-related elements of your business, and I withdraw myself from diving into what impact specific events in the world might have on your infrastructure, marketing, products, etc. From an HR perspective, it is pretty obvious that society as the outer circle of your organization creates unconsciously, unknowingly, or unintentionally an impact on the way you do business and the way you internally organize your business.

Here are some examples:

- Given the increase in terrorist threats and attacks, the feeling of security and safety becomes more than ever a primary hygiene factor (following Herzberg's theory on motivation) to consider. This impacts the HR health and safety policies related to limiting free access to your company premises, installing a access registration process and system for visitors.

- The recent immigration problems regarding masses of people moving into Western Europe, asking for asylum, has had an impact on what society looks like there. On the HR side, while working for an agency that provides services for people to facilitate integration in a new country, we were confronted with the immediate need to develop a policy for dealing with aggression from our customers toward our staff members.

- Increasing commuting times and traffic jams that do not seem to get resolved by better infrastructure necessitate rethinking the way to collaborate within your organization. You might come to the point of having to consider satellite offices to limit commuting time, or increase possibilities and associated investments and culture change to encourage more home working facilities. By going down these routes, you might just stay ahead of your competitors and create competitive advantages based upon a projected idea of what society will ask for in the years to come.

- The strong growth of e-business has pushed traditional companies (e.g., package industry, postal services) to strategically rethink their business model and the associated HR strategy implementation as a result of this. Finding ways to stay active and have staff work 24/7 is a massive change in labor conditions.

- When your local government introduces new legislation that pushes the legal retirement age up, so that people need to be able to continue working in conditions that are congruent with this new age limit, you might need to revisit your shift working policy.

2.2.2. Individual and Collective labor Law

Implementing HR and dealing with your employees is highly bound by legislative measures. Individual and collective labor law, or even broader social law, is an important and constituent element of the external environment that co-defines how you do business and what you can and cannot do in HR. It is a scientific discipline and needs specialists and experts to help you clarify what is allowed and what is not, taking into considerations geographical differences (i.e., the way you work with people in organizations located in San Diego is significantly different from in France or New Jersey).

Here are some examples:

- When aiming for maximal flexibility in your workforce, you might want to work with employment contracts of defined duration, to cover specific peaks in productivity. However, extending these contracts—e.g., due to a massive new sales order coming in—is not always legally possible.
- Some elements in your employment contract are fundamental and cannot be changed unilaterally, so when you operate in Belgium and an employee is noticeably more productive in another function than the one mentioned in the individual labor agreement, it requires a mutual and preferably written agreement to execute this function change.
- In some countries, it can be legally correct that an employer simply ends a labor agreement unilaterally, without having to justify his reasons, as long as the conditions to do so are respected, whereas in other countries, there is an important previous phase of gaining a government approval to let someone go.

Collective labor law is also highly different across countries and regions. In industrialized countries with a long history, you will see that the unions will have a strong voice in how to do business, specifically when working in industry. Services organizations will also need to respect social relations between employer and employee delegations, but the overall climate can be less stringent and more collaborative instead of combative. However, the processes and procedures described by collective labor law can be very stringent and suffocating at times. In this respect, it is of utmost importance that your HR leader understands the subtleties of this relationship, and does what it takes to develop a good and trustful partnership to ensure an effective collaboration.

Here are some examples:

- When you plan to restructure your organization, with a potential headcount cut as a result, you will need to be very vigilant and prepare upfront to fully respect all formal procedures, which differ across countries.
- Health and safety of your staff is a high focus of concern for the unions. Your social partners have an important authority and scope of responsibility towards jointly developing and monitoring health and preventing safety and security issues in your organization.

2.2.3. Labor Market

As a business leader, you need to know that HR operates thanks to or in spite of the **labor market**. The talents you need, the scarcity of them, the employees that are your ambassadors to the external world, and the specific offerings you develop to become an attractive employer are high differentiating factors worth investing in. Your image, the way you deal with your customers, your marketing, and the reports on business news will all influence your potential employees. Attracting, developing, and retaining high potentials, those people who will make your organization strive, is crucial for your company's success. In this arena, you will notice the velocity of talent, the scarcity and war for talent, and the impact of society on how future employees perceive your company as a potential employer.

Here are some examples:

- When you are in need of highly available talent, you might be able to easily recruit. However, retention can become an issue: you could end up recruiting at low cost, but with insufficient "tender love and care" afterwards, you might lose them to your competitor as soon as they have learned their profession at your expense.
- When you are looking for scarce talent, your company image will be highly important. You will need to go out there and actively promote yourself, your company, your products and what you can offer them, above and beyond what your competitors throw in.
- If you have invested heavily in attracting the best of the best (e.g., by offering internships and development opportunities to students, and recruiting them before they enter the labor market), but your internal organization is no good, or your management is not equipped to optimally support this generation or these specific high-potential new leaders, you will quickly see your investment go down the drain, with potentially devastating future negative effects on backfilling.

Also be aware that all these elements can mutually influence each other. When a local legislation requires each company of 100+ employees to invest in diversity (with fines and negative publicity if the expected diversity rate is not met), this might engender specific internal actions to live up to a newly created standard. You can choose to integrate the government-imposed measure into your own concern for diversity in your company vision, in this way becoming a strong advocate for diversity in the broadest sense of the word, and develop specific trainings and events to bring your diverse workforce into the spotlight to reinforce your company image to the outside world.

2.3. Stakeholders

Knowing how you ideally want HR to be set up and having identified key factors that will color your specific HR activities requires considering one other perspective. As a business leader, you know exactly what you want, and how and by when you want it. By now, you will have learned that this is not always as easy as it looks, because of the internal building blocks that might still need to be developed, and because of the external environment that might generate a number of limitations.

A final perspective to bring into this overall view is that of your **stakeholders**. What do they want, and why, and to what extent can you find common ground that is aligned with your own aspirations? Is there a way to find common denominators to develop a roadmap for standout HR that will be supported by all stakeholders, and that will be cherished and applauded by all of them? If your HR leader can end up finding a storyline, a vision, and a strategy to bring all stakeholders' perspectives together, thereby painting a future all can relate to, you can kiss the ground. This is what makes an HR leader really stand out: balancing different needs, aspirations and requests into one relatively simple yet appealing HR vision and strategy, considering all determining factors, and finding that unique combination of code that will make your HR unique, company-specific, and the engine to your company's success.

When we refer to stakeholders, we aim to look at and include many more parties than your official formal shareholders (those individuals or organizations that hold shares of your company). It is as the Business Dictionary describes it: a stakeholder is *"a person, group or organization that has interest or concern in an organization. Stakeholders can affect or be affected by the organization's actions, objectives and policies"* (http://www.businessdictionary.com/definition/stakeholder.html).

When defining your HR vision, strategy, and roadmap, make sure you include the many different types of stakeholders. Not only will they feel honored that you or your HR leader is taking the time and effort to listen to, understand, and include their point of view, but by including them in your quest for effective, company-original HR, you turn them into true and loyal ambassadors and supporters of your journey to success. They will become strong believers and will feel jointly responsible for the success of your endeavor, and they will do whatever you ask them to do because they were part of the initial inception of your Standout HR.

Most HR leaders and business leaders do include internal stakeholders to some extent in their analysis of the situation and in defining what Standout HR should look like in their organization. It is worthwhile to list the key internal stakeholders up front and include an interview or discussion with them prior to starting to develop your own HR perspective.

External parties are often forgotten. They can add important information and details to the overall picture developed by the internal stakeholders, and can bring an additional external perspective that can make the difference between a good and a Standout HR strategy. This is why we list both internal and external potential stakeholders.

2.3.1. Internal Stakeholders

It goes without saying that when developing Standout HR, the key team of the organization needs to be in the driving seat. This is not your HR department and its leader, but rather your management team—your direct reports, who have all mastered a part of your business and have been brought in to contribute to the success of your company.

Your **management committee** will usually have a pretty clear, yet potentially diverse, perspective on what HR should look like and how HR should differentiate and contribute to the company's success. They will need to jointly support and be able to justify HR decisions or impacts to the **board members and shareholders**. They, too, are important parties to include in a survey to determine the key driving forces to ensure organization success through HR interventions.

Your **supervisors, managers, and other people leaders** are another very important group of internal stakeholders to consider. They are heavily affected by what HR looks like within the organization, what processes are being developed, and to what extent they have impact and influence in the HR activities, as well as how it affects the way they can manage their people's team and individual performances.

In essence, when you think about it, your supervisors are your true and authentic HR managers. Day by day, they are managing their human resources; they are involved in and responsible for creating a strong, high-performing team. Among other duties, your supervisors are involved in the hiring process, they are the employees' coaches in many cases, they bring them up to speed, they spot development needs and approve trainings, they review and assess their contributions, and eventually they can have a say in salary increases, promotion potential or layoffs.

I can hear you ask, "But where does this leave my HR department, then?". Well, in my opinion, your HR department is the enabling factor; they make sure that supervisors can give their absolute best in coaching, managing, and developing their teams. HR facilitates, develops, and rolls out the correct tools and support so that people managers can shine in their people role, and individual employees can excel at what they do best.

HR is the toolbox, and is taking control of all operational activities that come with the job of working with people. HR needs to make sure that the employees and their managers don't have to worry about payroll, legislative requirements, and all transactional activities that are secondary to their focus of contributing to the team and the organization. HR is there to help and coach managers to give their very best and to provide all support needed to uplift every single individual employee. HR is providing the conditions to allow every individual to flourish. The way managers can and need to interact with their teams, and what they see as opportunities or obstacles, is crucial to integrate in the analysis for the creation of Standout HR.

The **employees** are also a stakeholder one should not neglect, not only because they usually outnumber all other stakeholders, but also because they can have a massive impact on the outlook and performance of your organization. It is not unexpected that people are called the "capital" of any organization. Regardless of the perspective through which you look at it—number of people and associated infrastructure, personnel cost, work processes related to employing people—without employees you have no organization, no thriving business, and no growing success.

Engaged employees, employees who feel good, who enjoy their work, their organization, their colleagues, and their management, are productive employees and their contribution to the net result will increase with their level of satisfaction and commitment. During the recent years, there is more and more talk about "happy people"; in some contexts, Happiness Officers are being created to make sure employees are happy. Though I do not think that this is the future, I do believe in including their perspectives and their aspirations to help make the organization a great place to be and to work for.

Specifically in larger organizations is the imminent need to question and relate to employees directly when developing a Standout HR. The distance between top management and the employee in the field grows, and they sometimes feel less connected to whatever management decides. When this disconnect takes bigger form, it will by default have a negative impact, both on the individual's wellbeing and on the organization's success.

Last but not least, let's not forget the fact that your employees are often also your customers so there is a double impact on your final numbers and net profit. If they are not fully engaged and committed, they will contribute less effectively and efficiently to your results, and they will probably feel less inclined to buy your products. On top of all this, they are also ambassadors to the outside world, attracting or scaring away future employees and thus, impacting your labor market, and also spreading news about your products, your business management, and your internal practices, impacting your sales, image, and external market.

When going through the internal stakeholders, let me finally spend a moment reflecting on your **social partners**, the unions and employee delegates that have a specific mandate to act as the voice of the employees and reside in a number of committees and formal organizations that are of bigger or lesser impact to your internal management. In many organizations, having to work with the unions is often mystified as hard and non-productive work, useless discussions that delay good progress and company growth. I do not adhere to this thinking. In my past experiences, I have had good and mediocre encounters with the unions.

In all circumstances, and on the condition that both parties mutually respect each other and take up the role they have gained through decades of industrial business life, I have always felt positively about developing a good, constructive, professional relationship between HR, employer representation, and the social partners. One can always find common ground, as long as there is authenticity in the collaboration and a joint final goal and destination. This is why it is important to include the social partners when thinking about what company-original HR should look like. And let there be no mistake, the unions can become your partner in crime. When the going gets tough, it does happen that by joining forces, magic can happen.

2.3.2. External Stakeholders

Involving external stakeholders in an analysis that should lead to the development of company-original, standout HR, is not something one spontaneously thinks about. And maybe this is the least crucial part of the survey phase that collects all stakeholder information to build your new HR. However, depending upon the nature of your business, the setup, and the way external parties can contribute interesting perspectives about differentiating your organization, it might be useful to at least give it some reflection and make a thought-out decision as to whether or not to include them in your survey.

STANDOUT HR • 68

The first group of external stakeholders you might consider are your **external partners and vendors**. The companies you do business with, your suppliers, might have their own perception of your organization and what—in their view—it would take to rise above mediocrity. One example of an external partner that can bring in valuable information, since it is part of your internal processing, could be your catering service provider. They usually have contact with lots of people within your organization, because they come across multiple projects and need to align to internal processes. They have an external view from the inside of your organization.

The same can be argued for **external consultants** that are being brought in temporarily in specific parts of the organization. They, too, can bring valuable input. If you are working with a marketing agency, you can include their opinion based upon what they see about how the external world responds to your organization. Trainers, gardeners, and security people are all external parties that might have something interesting to add. Again, they will very much appreciate you asking for their opinions.

The **government** is hardly ever included as an external stakeholder, but it is worth considering. Perhaps you are servicing the government, or you might be seen as a role model, exemplary in applying an original approach to issued governmental regulations, or maybe you are calling upon government officials, government subsidies, or government services. There can be interesting intersections with your business that could make it worthwhile to broach the topic of developing a standout HR during one of the planned business meetings; it does not even have to be more than this. But by simply sharing this practice with them, they might remember it in the future and recommend you as a sparring partner for some speaking gig.

Finally, another external stakeholder that can provide interesting perspectives is your **competition**, companies working in the same space you do, suffering from the same diseases and problems, finding solutions to common problems, etc. They, too, can shed some light on possible challenges or opportunities to consider in developing your company-original HR. They can voice what former employees, vendors, and candidates tell them about you, and can share the image they have about how you operate internally and what you show externally.

2.4. The Company-Original HR model Overview

Adding now all additional factors that influence how the generic model should operate to make it company-original and reflect the specificity of your organization, the more detailed model can be visualized in the below overview. The next step is to discern how to analyse these influences and translate the basic HR model into a company-specific model for your organization is the next step to engage in. More about this in the following section.

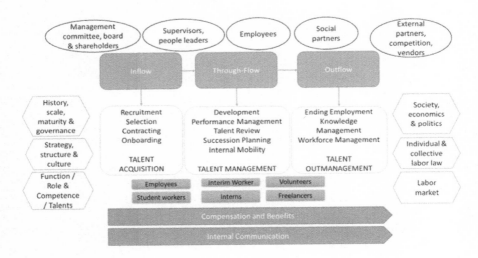

SECTION 3:

ROADMAP TO
COMPANY-ORIGINAL HR

Bringing the basic and generic HR model together with organization-specific internal building blocks and key differentiating external factors will shed some light on what your company-original HR should look like. Collecting your stakeholders' input and bringing all this into a final meta-analysis of what, in your specific situation, HR should look like, is taking the highway to effective, efficient and standout HR.

Nothing less but standout HR should be your ambition because it provides the direct link to **key organizational performance**: it will set the scene for continuous **organization development and change** and it will allow for **organization agility** in internal processes and self-regulation. The **engagement** level of your employees will skyrocket and your overall **employability** will be at an all-time high, setting your organization for long-term success, productivity, growth, and profit. The underlying **organization culture** will be tremendously strong and ready to face any and every future challenge or adversity.

Below, you can find a visual representation of all these elements: basic HR model, internal building blocks, external influences, key stakeholders, and organizational performance indicators. This visual is highly helpful whenever talking about your company's challenges and opportunities. For every business discussion, there is undoubtedly an HR angle, and using this overview to see where and how HR can play its role is extremely useful.

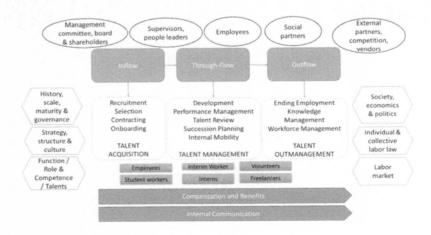

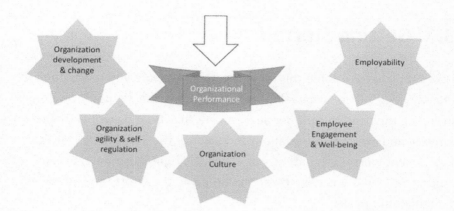

The final action to initiate is to bring it all together in a roadmap to inventorize all information from all angles, analyze it into a solid proposal, and roll out this new company-original HR. In this section, you will find the inspiration and "how-to's" to get started: Who you should involve and in what phase, what tools you should use, what process you should follow, how to define the specific assignment and expected outcome, how to govern the process from start to finish, etc. Next, I will describe in more detail what the process looks like, what to engage in, what and how to plan all activities, and how to assess and monitor progress and outcome. I will share with you some of the tools I usually use to help you with the project set-up, data collection, and analysis. Finally, I've added some lessons, attention points, tips and tricks, so that you can take advantage of my own experiences and set yourself for imminent success.

As a bonus, I have included a case study. You will find the very first company-original HR report I ever wrote, many years ago for my first customer, covering the analysis of the business leaders' input as key to the development and proposal of a new business embedded HR.

3.1. Getting Started

Now that you have come this far in the book, I'm sure you understand the endeavor you face to develop and implement the right HR strategy—including the need to consider all company-specific and company-relevant internal and external information, and balance the aspirations of different key stakeholders. Fortunately, you are in the right place now, because as a business leader you have taken the time and the effort to learn the very fundamentals of HR.

There are a couple of key questions you need to answer when getting geared up: How to determine who will lead the project, how to define the assignment, scope, and expected outcomes, and how to set up basic but effective governance, including communication related to this project.

3.1.1. Who Will Lead the Project?

I have previously argued that HR is an activity of every supervisor, it should be at the heart and mind of every key business and people leader. However, this does not imply that you should take this project on your shoulders. You will be the **key sponsor** of this project, the one who can make a crucial decision if need be, but you need a leader to manage the building and development of a company-original, Standout HR. You have multiple options to consider:

- Appoint *your current HR leader* to manage, lead, and achieve this project

  This is a valuable option, and a pretty safe one as well. There are a number of advantages to asking your own HR leader to take this project to fruition: he or she knows the company, and should be able to identify those internal building blocks to take into account when developing your standout HR. Your current HR leader is familiar with today's strategy and practices within HR and the impact it has on your business. He or she knows who can be considered representative spokespersons for your different stakeholder groups.Another advantage is that your HR leader can both develop the company-original HR and oversee its efficient rollout and implementation.

However, there are a number of downsides. In the first place, he should have gone down this route of developing a company-original, Standout HR a long time ago, if he was competent and proficient in the HR field, so maybe he does not have the right skillset to initiate and drive such a project. Also, if he has never managed such a project before, he might be stretched to bring this to success, which is a stress factor not to overlook. Even if there are no competency issues, and you have all faith and confidence in your current HR leader, you still might want to consider someone else for two other specific reasons.

The first reason is that you need a captain on board to ensure business as usual continues and your operations do not suffer any fallback from investing to heavily in this project. The HR department as it currently works and operates needs to be able to continue delivering the same level of service to your organization as before. Your incumbent HR leader needs to have his head clear to provide this continued guidance to his team and to the rest of the organization.

The second reason is that the outcome of the analysis phase might reveal the need for drastic change. A sitting HR leader is usually not very much in favor of disruptive actions, of significantly changing the existing *modus operandi* and diverting strongly from the path walked with so much conviction up to now.

- *Use the momentum when introducing **a new HR leader***

If by chance you are in the situation (or soon will be) that your current HR leader will leave or has left recently, or will take on pension or another role outside HR or outside of your company, it might be the best possible moment for a new leader to board and launch his new role with this project. This is what happens in many situations. A new HR leader joining an organization is bound to start by taking an initial period (usually up to three months) to dive into the generic model and all surrounding context to develop his own HR strategy.

The downside is that usually, this will not be done as thoroughly and in depth as you would want, simply because there is high pressure on this new HR leader to start delivering, to demonstrate the reason he or she was hired in the first place, and to very quickly realize a number of visible changes that will give the rest of the organization the basic level of comfort that he or she was a good choice to join. Moreover, this new leader will need to keep the fort up and running, in combination with learning about the company and developing his or her idea of the best company-based HR strategy. That is a lot of weight to put on one person's shoulders.

- *Assign the project to a **high potential from within** the organization with strong HR affinity or knowledge*

  This can be a great option, if all conditions for success are met. It could really be a very authentic demonstration of the business' conviction to call upon internal talent to develop the future. It shows a strong commitment to development of your people. If you have this possibility, make sure to chaperon this person vigilantly, have him or her report directly into you, and be as close as you can to protect, monitor, coach, and guide wherever desirable.

  Make sure you have found a common understanding with your standing HR leader so that he or she does not feel threatened and fully supports this as well. He or she needs to see the absolute benefits of this approach; if not, do not initiate it. Finally, make sure your entire management committee is in favor of and actively supports the sponsorship. The person identified who has agreed to take this project should be released from his own activities and obligations to fully concentrate on the project and on his interactions with the rest of the organization.

  If your organization is ready for this approach, you should embrace it and exploit it to the fullest. And if proven successful, I can guarantee that fellow management committee members will raise their hand to have someone do the same thing for their own strategy development. This can generate an entire movement of talent, energy, reflection, innovation, and evolution in your organization.

- *Hire an **external HR leader***

A final option to consider is bringing HR from the outside in, to turn your HR inside out. This is my personal favorite, but it is again up to your own sense of what is best for your organization, given its specific constellation and timing, to consider all pros and cons of the different options.

There are multiple benefits in asking external help to perform this analysis and develop a proposal for a company-original, Standout HR. Bringing in an external specialist buys you time, energy, expertise, new perspectives, focus, and the courage to decide on a new future, however disruptive this may be for the residing HR department and for the organization. The expertise he or she brings in can outweigh the lack of an internal network. It is easier for an external leader with a blank, unprecedented, unbiased look to recognize how things and people relate, or how things can clash.

An external HR leader who has done this kind of project before can rely on his or her previous experiences and accelerate significantly the processes of setting up the project, going through all the different phases, and proposing and deciding on a final new original HR. He can add content, innovative thinking and problem solving because of his familiarity with what is out there in the external world.

An external leader can focus on this project without any distractions from today's operational and transactional concerns or necessities. He or she can bring in all outside expertise related to HR, including experiences in comparable companies, and can easily and without risk of being internally blamed or damaged turn the existing HR strategy and practices inside-out. It is easier for an external person to have a fresh and unbiased look at current HR, comment on or criticize its current status, and present alternative options than it is for an internal leader to do so. We all know that assigning an external HR leader comes with a price, but in my experience, it is heavily worth it in terms of efficacy, efficiency, and spot-on analyses that identify and quickly cure flaws and inadequacies in the system.

3.1.2. Defining Assignment, Scope, and Expected Outcomes

Irrespective of the choice you make in terms of who will lead the project of developing a company-original, Standout HR, it is of crucial importance to outline the assignment as specifically as possible, making sure that the scope is clear, well-defined, and agreed upon by your key sponsors, and that the expected outcomes are clearly described both in terms of results and output, and in terms of timing of final outcome delivery.

I usually work with a three-step approach. First, it is up to the sponsor, you as business leader, to **define the boundaries and expected returns** of this project. You should think about it as specifically as possible and after revision and discussion with your management committee and possibly your board members (your key sponsors), you should develop a draft project charter that states the name, objective, key milestones, participants, budget, expected timing, and details on outcomes and results. This initial project charter will be the basis for explaining the mission or assignment to whomever will be requested to take the lead and manage the project from kick-off to termination and internal handover to operational implementation.

Next, the project manager will **refine and further elaborate the initial project charter** to make sure it is fully understood and captures all necessary elements to make a final joint decision to move forward. Elements that will likely be added relate to number and specific capabilities of people involved in specific subtasks or -processes, specific tools and templates for reporting purposes, overall governance throughout the project, risk assessment and mitigations, estimated budget and billable days or hours needed by key project team members, prior preparation in terms of training the project team members and communication moments, channels, and tools, etc. This extended project charter will then need to be **agreed upon and formally approved** by the sponsor team prior to kick-off.

3.1.3. Setting Up Governance and Communication

A well-developed project charter usually covers at least high-level project governance. However, in my experience it is worthwhile to spend specific time and concentration discussing up-front the best and most effective governance of this project with your sponsor team, your project leader, his or her team, and if desirable, other parties (e.g., social partners or external stakeholders).

You should at least take the time to agree on who should be involved in project status meetings, informal updates on process, progress and content discussions, and additional "alert" meetings when decisions need to be made related to time, money, scope, and risks linked to the project rollout. Once the who and what" is agreed upon, discuss and block out specific time slots in each other's calendars for these periodic meetings and formally agree to not cancel them or decline participation unless for explicit, justified reasons. Agree on delegation procedures s in case of emergencies that prevent people from participating. Make sure that the rules of the game are abundantly clear to everyone, so that no time is lost when decisions are made during these meetings that might get revoked later on due to someone's absence.

Finally, and most importantly, take time to discuss communication. None of us has ever said not to worry about communication. Every single one of us doing business and involved in processes that link to change, management, innovation, data collection and interpretation, proposal discussions, etc., knows and understands the importance of communication. Yet, all of us, at the end of a project and looking back at key learnings, will at some point bring up communication. It is the one thing that can turn a great project in a massive failure or lost opportunity.

So, if we at least understand one thing, it's that it is imperative to discuss communication before the start of the project, and include a communication section in every single aspect of activity related to the project. In every report, status update, meeting, or get together, make sure that communication is part of the agenda.

What I have experienced as a good approach is to actively involve and give a strong voice and mandate to a communications expert right from the beginning, through to the end (and beyond). I am aware that it is not doable to have communications involved in everything that happens in an organization, but when we are in the midst of questioning our HR strategy and involving multiple stakeholders, dedicating a project team to work on developing this company-original, Standout HR, it goes without saying that this is highly sensitive to every single employee.

A communications expert can help you develop a communication strategy so that your staff is informed, clear, interested in this project, and committed to learn about the progress and results. The dynamics that you initiate by setting up a specific communication strategy, with diverse channels, speakers, contents, formats, multidirectional communications, etc., will provide the proper climate and setting for this project to evolve and come to fruition in a climate of trust, openness, and dialogue.

It is very much like any activity involving change: sufficient time and attention dedicated to talking, listening, dialoguing, and communicating will set the scene for success. When you can provide a communications plan at the outset, expectations are set that need to be met, and it will also allow you to refer to this plan so that chaotic communications and messages floating around all over the place can be avoided, and serenity throughout the project can be maintained.

3.2. Process

The process to bring this kind of project to fruition includes a number of phases, blocks of activity that can be distinguished. I usually refer to them as follows: setting the scene, preparation, data collection, data analysis and results description, proposal development and finalization, and implementation.

3.2.1. Setting the Scene

Setting the scene encompasses many of the activities mentioned above. It is all about making sure that all conditions are met and enabled for a good project plan rollout. During this phase, the project charter is being developed and finalized, the project governance structure is being set up and validated, the communication strategy is set out, and the infrastructure, logistical, and technology needs are being clarified.

3.2.2. The Preparation Phase

The preparation phase comprises those activities that are launched and finalized prior to coming to the first key action of the project, the data collection. In this phase, the **project team** is set up, and all members are approached and introduced to the project charter and to their roles and responsibilities. They are being trained with the tools and methodology that will be applied during this project.

In this context it is important to respect the key activities necessary to build a team. I very gratefully refer here to the extensive research and model of Bruce Tuckman, covering the five stages of team development[3]. (Tuckman and Jensen, 1977). This model can serve as a framework to use when forming and coaching the team during this project. Project team members will be responsible for the following activities, among other

---

[3] These stages are: forming, storming, norming, performing, adjourning

things: administrative support, interviewers, interview note-takers, communication contacts, data extraction specialists, data analysts, HR members, and business members.

Next to the project team members, the **project participants** will be defined, selected, requested for participation, and briefed about their role in the project. Those participants come from all identified stakeholders that the sponsor team has decided to include in the project.

Finally, a **formal kick-off meeting** with everyone involved is an important milestone. This meeting serves to bring everybody together (sponsors, project team, project participants), create the eagerness to get started, answer all remaining questions and address open topics, and serve as inspiration to the overall project related communication strategy within the organization.

3.2.3. Data Collection and Inventory

The first explicit activity of the project team is **the data collection and inventory phase**. When looking back at my experiences in managing these projects, depending upon what specific data are most relevant to this specific situation, I usually end up with a limited set of data collection methods.

Funnel Based Interviewing (FBI) key stakeholders has always been my most important and highly used method, generating heaps of valuable and interesting qualitative information. This FBI technique applies a specific format, identical across every single interviewee, using the same methodology and approach over and over again. This is also part of the training during the preparation phase. The interview format is strict, binding, and following a very specific strategy to allow the interviewee to discuss what is most dear and familiar to him or her, and his or her own objectives, perceptions and realities.

Slowly, by utilizing the exact questioning the interviewers have learned to apply, the interviewee is drilled down via a funnel method into HR aspects. The interviewer is fully focused on the dialogue and on extracting information, whereas the note-taker records all information to the maximum extent possible, literally writing down exactly what is being said by the interviewee using pen and paper, to avoid the disturbing noise of typing on a keyboard. Moreover, writing things down requires the brain to think more and thus be more focused to the content. In some cases it can be proposed to record the interview to transcribe later on; this might save some resources and time, but I have experienced it being somewhat less effective in this context. I have seen some people displaying resistance or discomfort, or withhold information, when they know they are being recorded.

Facilitated and guided workshops with key business people can be another valuable method of collecting information related to the internal building blocks that need to be taken into account to customize the standard HR practices and tools. Discussing strategy, systems, culture, and the organization's maturity and life cycle can and will generate interesting and valuable insights to translate to input for your new company-original HR.

Quantitative data collection related to HR metrics can also be important additional information to include in the full data collection phase. These data can relate to employees' demographic characteristics, key indicators in terms of turnover, absences, leaves, promotion ratio, time to fill vacancies, etc. ...

3.2.4. Data Analysis and Results Description

Bringing all data together and jumping into the **data analysis and results description phase** is where you bring music to the notes. The ultimate goal here is to distill the common denominators that are consistent across all data sources. I remember when I started to analyze the interviews, I read through all transcripts out loud and highlighted the key elements, bringing it all together to post to a "wall of information" to see if there was a story to tell, looking at the answer to each question across all stakeholders to find the common ground or the key disparities. Disparities and common thinking were then cross-analyzed with quantitative data, with the answers to other similar or contradictory questions. If you take the time to bring it all together and visualize it on a huge board or wall, you will start seeing things, you can start grouping, ungrouping, linking, ordering, and highlighting until the basic message becomes apparent.

Next, the project team has the task of finding a way to comprehensively describe the results in order to feedback to the participants and highlight key outcomes. This seems easy, but the biggest pitfall here is that when describing the results, one starts interpreting information and building conclusions. Important nuances might get lost and opinions might get pushed one direction or another. The ultimate goal of this phase is to allow the participant to take note of what came out of the data collection, pure and unprejudiced raw data, but in a condensed and structured way. This overview then needs to be communicated to, discussed with, and validated by the project participants.

In many cases this step is often overlooked and the project team jumps right into the development and presentation of key conclusions and the translation into a proposal for a renewed HR strategy. By doing so, you risk losing your audience and your stakeholders because they might lack insight in how you moved from their input and your data analysis to your conclusions. This is opening the door to collective resistance and non-acceptance, potentially even rejection of buy-in to the end result, with the argument that their input was not even taken into account. So make sure to plan this intermediate feedback session so that people can understand and learn about the key results, provide additional context and even launch a number of suggestions for how to move forward.

3.2.5. Proposal Development

The final step in this project is the **proposal development and finalization**. The feedback session is an important milestone. During this session you gain agreement and buy-in with the results collected, and can see how it all relates and can come together in a company-original, Standout HR. During this session, proposals and suggestions will come to the table, and participants will feel very much involved in translating all these results in the "now what?" scenario building. With this input, the project team can develop the masterpiece and create a proposal for how to define and provide content to a company-original, Standout HR, linked to the key outcomes of business challenges and opportunities,as well as how HR can play its role in helping to overcome obstacles and achieve the business strategy.

Usually, one can start with identifying those current things within HR that go against the renewed thinking. These elements can easily be captured and removed. This is the first step. It is easier to identify what your HR is not, before you can start thinking about what it should become. Next, it's important to think about those things that are truly very bold and obvious, coming out of the data analysis, that should be your core and centerpiece of Standout HR. Identifying this, giving it an appealing name or phrase, and translating this into every single aspect of your HR practice is the cornerstone of your proposal.

This proposal should then first be shared with the sponsor team to check for business coherence, attractiveness, and feasibility. Next, the proposal should be introduced to the HR team, specifically to include their input, but also to start the change process with the understanding that the company-original, Standout HR will only stand out if they make it real. Next to the business leaders and key stakeholders, the entire HR team will need to buy in to this to the full extent, take ownership and accountability, and find the drive and appetite to make this their future. With these two key checkpoints, the sponsor team and HR team validating and formally and full-heartedly buying in, the proposal is ready for communication and implementation.

STANDOUT HR • 86

3.2.6. Implementation

Implementation implies that the overall agreed-upon strategy, vision, key focus areas, and new direction are being translated into specific action plans, goals, and objectives to define, allocate, and achieve. This part of the work should be handed over to the HR leader. He or she will now be owner of this company-original HR. He or she will have as a key objective to make this renewed HR come to life and generate standout business results. There is now a clear and distinct path to success, with explicit expectations translated into action plans. This now has to become part of the operational functioning of the HR team. The project leader should be at ease to hand over the implementation plan, and to close the project down.

During implementation, and knowing that this usually is a process that will take multiple years to accomplish, the HR leader can now see this as a change process, and initiate as many "Plan-Do-Check-Act" cycles as he or she can handle, so that every new subproject, or launch of renewed HR practice can follow the Plan, Do, Check and Act approach to make it happen. The HR leader will also need to manage expectations and develop a plan to demonstrate how he or she will make it happen, one step at a time, but moving forward consistently. Providing periodic status updates and developing the right set of key performance indicators, as well as a dashboard to visualize progress, will keep the renewed HR going and will eventually lead to Standout HR.

On the counter side, as a business leader, you will now need to check and monitor the effects and impact this renewed company-original HR will generate on identified business outcomes and business improvement or growth indicators.

3.3. Tools

When you hire an external HR consultant to manage this project, he will most probably have his own tools that will be used to facilitate this project. For completeness, I can give you some highlights around what I have found extremely useful when running this type of project.

3.3.1. Project Charter

The success of your project partly depends upon a solid and joint understanding of what the specific scope of the project is, the expected outcome for key deliverables, and the underlying objectives, timelines, resources, and budgets. Take sufficient time to get this written down, discussed with sponsors, key stakeholders and the project team prior to launching the project. There are multiple templates available that serve exactly this purpose. Do not hesitate to try out multiple formats to check which one is most applicable and easy to use and refer to.

Make sure that this **project charter** document is *the* go-to document whenever discussions arise about scope, depth of analysis, people involved, etc. Keep it readily available and start every progress meeting with this charter to keep focus constantly remind everyone what you are doing, why and how, so that everyone involved is on the same page. Also, in the case of other people joining the project team or the organization, use this project charter as the starting point to get them quickly and effectively on board and up to speed.

3.3.2. Data Collection – Interview Canvas

There are multiple data sources one can access when collecting all required specific information to develop an organization's company-original, Standout HR.

The novelty that I have always brought to the table lies in the **interview canvas** I have used on multiple occasions to question business leaders and other business stakeholders. I strongly believe that the way this interview canvas is set up, and the structure it offers to move from business-related areas all the way down to HR specifics, is the differentiating factor in my approach for collecting information that will determine what HR should look like. Credit goes to Valerie Schoenfelder, external consultant, who introduced me to the concept and usage, and who trained me to incorporate the rationale, the execution, and the analysis of the captured information.

As I described earlier, the interviews with business stakeholders are crucial. I always have an interviewer who focuses exclusively on the interviewee and on extracting all information possible, concentrating on the content while paraphrasing and asking for extra clarification. The note-taker is responsible for recording the interviewee's exact word choices. These interviews usually take a minimum of two hours, often more, and are energy draining for all three persons present and active, as this activity is highly focused and in-depth. This is necessary to reach the true essence and fundamentals of what the interviewee is bringing up. This is exactly where the benefits of the developed interview protocol step in.

This interview protocol covers 19 questions which are used in a standard and undeviating order. During the initial training, the interviewer learns why every single question is important, and what to look for when asking each question. The first seven questions relate exclusively to the interviewee's goals, dreams, challenges, needed and/or received support, frustrations, the way his or her team operates, etc. During these seven questions, all reference to HR-related information should be avoided at all times. It is only after these questions have been asked that the interviewer narrows the subject matter down to HR, but only referring to HR from the specific business context that has been revealed in the previous seven questions.

When all questions have been discussed, the final question is another crucial one, often forgotten. It is the broadest question, asking if the interviewee has any questions. Believe it or not, this is an easy question to forget—but please don't. It is the interviewee's turn to ask a few questions, and some people feel more comfortable if you "give permission".

This is also the point where you formally and explicitly close your notebook. This is the moment when some amazing things can come up, once the person has the perception that the interview is done. Do not write anything down at this point, but instead listen extremely carefully and openly, and do note the key messages in your summary session afterwards. Valuable information can be generated this way and added to your overall picture. This interview protocol, and the rationale behind and how-to related to each question, is available upon simple demand. At the beginning and end of this book, there is a page where you can simply click through to request a free copy of this interview protocol.

3.3.3. Template Report

There are many ways to report back to your sponsor team regarding the key findings and results. The justification of your proposal for a renewed company-original, Standout HR can take on multiple formats. I have always chosen to present a comprehensive description of the project, including the project charter, process gone through, and key people/functions involved.

An overview of the key findings is at the basis of the report, making sure that the sponsor team and stakeholders can relate to the outcome and recognize certain info without losing any anonymity. The key findings can be grouped in multiple ways depending upon the situation, audience, etc. The core of the report is then the translation of the key findings into a framework proposal for a renewed company-original HR. Finally, this can be further drilled down to some key HR objectives to bring the proposal to realization and to set the basics for a further project implementation roadmap.

At the end of this section, I have added a bonus, a copy of a similar project I did where I interviewed business leaders using the above-discussed interview protocol, went through the analysis, discussed the results, and developed a new HR proposal.

Next to such a report, I always create a highly visual and attractive PowerPoint presentation to allow for the story behind it to come to life. This story will then be the basis for any further and upcoming communications throughout the organization and during the months and even years to come when HR, in collaboration with the business, is implementing this new HR strategy into the day-to-day practice.

3.4. Key Learnings and Takeaways

You have now gained insight in the overall process to go through when you have decided to take on a project leader, team, and participants to step away from generic, basic HR and move towards a company-original Standout HR. You might have felt at some point a bit overwhelmed with the amount of information, the depth of analyses and discussions, the absolute need for creativity and innovation, and the unexpected outcome it might generate.

Indeed, this is a impactful way to proceed and is stepping out of the ordinary, the normal day-to-day operational way of doing business. Here lies another reason to leave this in the hands of those who know exactly what they are doing, due to the expertise gained in previous multiple, diverse situations. But having come this far in my book, I do want to share with you some of my key learnings and takeaways.

3.4.1. Think Twice Before Jumping In

Hold your horses! This advice is crucial to prevent failure right from the start, as soon as you feel the urge to develop a company-original HR. It happens so frequently that business leaders like you—after having read the above sections—feel that they understand why their HR is not what it should be, and want to take immediate action to start criticizing the current HR strategy and practices, thereby potentially doing more harm than good.

Developing a company-original HR is not simply throwing away the "as-is" situation and doing something new. The only way to successfully move from a generic HR to this kind of customized HR is by taking the time to go through a period of reflection, thoroughly thinking through your own business, your goals, your aspirations, and your challenges prior to projecting this toward HR initiatives that can help you in your business journey to growth and success.

It is important to keep in mind that updating your HR model will take your organization through change and transformation, something that cannot happen overnight. There are countless books written about the process and psychology of change, so it is important to remember that change takes time, preparation, resilience, and perseverance. John Kotter, one of my gurus, developed an easy-to-adopt model when guiding organizations through a change process (*Leading Change, Kotter J, 1996*). As you most likely understood from the above description of the project's process, you will need to analyze sufficiently before moving into the action part of the project. Having to go back because of a lack of analysis is deadly to the success of this kind of project.

3.4.2. The Plight of Overanalysis

The opposite of the above is that a business leader, management team, or project team might feel overwhelmed and paralyzed from taking action, given the extent of the impact they are likely to generate on the company's day-to day-life. We all know that we can continue analyzing until eternity; there is always another point of view to include, another set of data to compare, another perspective to explore.

This project, developing a company-original HR that can stand out and provide your business with the strategic injection it needs to move the needle in terms of growth, needs a defined end date. This is why it is so crucial to decide and agree upon specific timings up front. Time is needed to set everything up, to collect all the information you think is valuable, needed, and useful, and to bring it all together for analysis.

Make sure you set the date for the meeting where the results of the data analyses will be shared with all participants and do not allow any deviation from that date. This meeting is, by far, the scariest of all meetings during this entire project, but it is the one that needs to take place to create the momentum to move forward into the proposal development. There is nothing worse than spending numerous hours and calling upon numerous people to help you collect the data when in the end, nothing comes out because nobody has the courage to stop the analysis phase.

As scary as it might be, according to Chandler Bolt[4], "Done is always better than perfect." Perfection is an illusion, but greatness is possible if you allow yourself to say, "This is as good and complete as it gets at this moment." Refining later on or adding points and commas at a later stage for improvement is a far better approach than trying to achieve perfection and analysing until eternity without acting on your results.

3.4.3. Quick Wins and Pilots

When you finally agree on what your company-original HR should look like and you make explicit what needs to be initiated, developed, and changed to move from your begin-state to your end-state, your HR department will most probably be paralyzed with the magnitude of the endeavour. Cutting it to digestible pieces, developing a roadmap and starting small, is an approach that works. It provides comfort to those who need to implement the change, it provides a perspective to those who can hardly wait to see it all happening, and it gives a road ahead to translate into a specific journey. This roadmap has a number of stops: moments to celebrate achievements along the way, and moments to stop and reflect on where your organization is heading and if it is still on track. Starting small with delivering some quick wins is a proven way to develop success and strong faith in the future, and demonstrate that change is really happening.

Pilots are another great way of changing softly. I remember when I needed to introduce the "strengths-based" approach to include identification of talents and strengths of an individual as important input for career guidance and planning. My HR team was very enthused and eager to get this going, and all of them knew that there was high demand, but none of my team members were familiar with the technique.

---

[4] Chandler Bolt, CEO of Self Publishing School, often refers to this phrase when urging students to continue moving forward towards completion and publication of their book.

So, prior to launching this to the organization in terms of an HR service we would offer to employees, we set up a pilot in two ways. I applied the strengths-based identification technique to some of my team members so that they could experience it themselves, and could develop great insight into what an employee is expected to gain and how HR could proactively make it part of the offering. Next, I trained a team member to experiment with this method with one or two employees that already had been reaching out to HR for career guidance. This way, the HR team could pilot this service, gain confidence around it, and also assess the time and resources needed to further deploy this within the organization.

Another pilot I used to verify if a new approach would work was to bring all vacancy management to the central head office of a particular company, where similar vacancies could be handled exactly the same way irrespective of where the position was located. This meant using the same standards regarding interviewing processes and techniques, so that the head office would propose good candidates to the local HR partners and hiring managers for validation and approval. There was initially quite some resistance; it felt to some like giving away power or independence, but taking advantage of the economy of scale, we could operate more quickly and effectively, leading to satisfaction from both the hiring managers across the country as well as the HR people involved in the process. This positive assessment of the pilot led to the introduction of this way of acquiring talent as the new standard approach.

3.4.4. Underpromise and Overdeliver

Usually, when the birth of your company-original Standout HR is being announced and explained in terms of how this will change and improve life at your organization, the expectations will skyrocket. Remember that you have included multiple stakeholders, all having potentially different expectations as to what should happen first and what is key to start with. Some of them will even argue that all novelties will need to take place immediately, and there should be a breach of the old and a birth of the new that is very transformational but has a disruptive effect on the organization's growth, success, and business results. You might even feel like this yourself!

As urgent as it might look now to really get going, and as tempting as it is to throw out the old to replace with the new Standout HR, practice prudence. Make sure that you do not set up your HR department for ultimate failure because of the urgency of wanting it all right now. Your HR leader will need to set the correct expectations and to negotiate with the sponsor team and eventually with key stakeholders to agree upon how to get started, focusing on one or a couple of new initiatives to develop prior to moving into the next set of changes. It is always better to agree up front that you cannot do it all at once, and to start with some humble first targets to achieve. This will temper the pressure and allow for the possibility of "business as usual" while developing new HR, and can lead to HR achieving more than initially agreed upon—hence, overdelivering.

What boosts motivation and is more inspiring than performing better and faster and more than agreed upon with key customers? So, underpromise slightly but overdeliver highly, gaining confidence from both the actors and the receivers and setting up the best possible momentum and dynamics for continued growth and change.

3.4.5. KPI and Dashboard

On many occasions, it has become more and more a habit to define a number of **key performance indicators** (KPI's) and group them on a dashboard for regular updates and periodic review during progress meetings. This practice, however, is mostly seen to support and monitor the project progress. It is less a habit to define these at the launch of project implementation. As a key learning, I would advise you to also take a moment to reflect upon the specific content of a project implementation dashboard, a dashboard with a number of KPI's that provide guidance in terms of progress toward final implementation of all related initiatives. Remember that during project management, the focus is mostly on **progress updates** with some key indicators related to this, whereas during project implementation, focus needs to move to **outcomes updates and tracking**.

A diversified dashboard, covering both progress and outcome, is also a great communication tool for the rest of your organization and a perfect instrument to keep all separate workgroups involved in various projects informed about their own and their colleagues' progress. The only thing I should warn you about is to make sure that this dashboard is nothing more than a means to an end, and not an end *per se*. The dashboard is instrumental in keeping the momentum going, in not losing sight of the end game, and in staying focused and on track, but it is the results, and the way of approaching the end goals, that matter most.

Finally, share successes, and celebrate them, but also share failure and learn from it. As I recently learned in reading Scott Allan's *Empower Your Life*, obstacles have one of 5 specific purposes, and they are roadblocks that are in essence tools for development and growth—so embrace them, rather than avoiding them!!

BONUS:

A HEALTHCARE COMPANY CASE

This book has served to explain that it is not so difficult to develop an HR strategy that optimally supports you in your business and organizational development. I hope that it has become clear that HR cannot be a standalone discipline, a take-it-off-the-shelf practice, a generic process applicable in all circumstances, contexts, sectors, and organizations. On the contrary, if you want HR to pay off, to deliver on the promise, and to make it worth the investment, you need to make sure that your HR strategy is company-original and breathes your organization's values, culture, language, and aspirations.

By doing so, you create the conditions to have Standout HR, and this is what HR is all about. You want to stand out with your business, so it's important to have your HR strategy stand out, too. HR touches every single individual contributor to your business' growth; if it does not stand out in the eyes of your employees, your competitors, and your shareholders, you are destined for failure.

This entire book is focused on explaining how to develop a company-original, Standout HR, and provides a clear roadmap with additional tools that are ready to use. In the next section, I have included a report that I wrote to propose a company-original, Standout HR for a healthcare company I was working for at that time. This was a medium-sized company with about 600 employees, a subsidiary of a global organization. The company was successful, but missed the spark to truly stand out, to employees, future employees, customers, and the local healthcare authorities.

Within HR, we were asked to reflect upon ourselves, to reinvent our department given that we did not really prove to be indispensable but rather a pain in the overall collaboration with our internal customers. At the time, we were seen more as a cost factor than as a go-to partner in driving the organization to success. So in the next section I explain how we went about interviewing stakeholders, analysing results, and developing a company-original HR that was further refined by translating it into a limited set of new HR objectives. This was the birth of building Standout HR.

The report structure reflects the process gone through, from project outline, to key business leaders' input, to developing a comprehensive framework and proposal for company-original HR which was ultimately translated into four key short-term HR goals. And this was finally turned into a Standout HR framework.

The report can be found below, in its original form. Read is as if you were a senior manager, that is being introduced to the outcomes of the project. This report is being made available for further communication within the organization.

Introduction

The HR function within our company is at a turning point for introducing important changes in the way it is supporting the business. With the arrival of a new Head of HR Department, a new wind has already been noticed and felt both within and outside the HR Department.

Given important changes in the external and internal environment, HR cannot sit back and expect not to be subject to similar changes. On the contrary, if HR wants to play the role it should play and wants to earn a seat at the table, it will need to demonstrate its value to the business; it will need to be at the forefront of change and help drive the business to its maximum performance. To do so, we've set up a project that would guide us through a process of learning about and gaining insight in business needs, business expectations, and current HR strengths and weaknesses, while at the same time confronting the way HR as a team operates.

The expected outcome of this exercise is twofold. First, based upon a thorough understanding of how HR can genuinely support the business in achieving its goals, it will lead to a solid HR strategy with associated HR objectives to translate that strategy into reality. This HR strategy, being a result of an internal business survey, will be closely aligned to the key business priorities and will thus contribute to the future of our company and the overall success of our business. We are more specifically aiming to present a company-original HR that will stand out from what it was before and from our competitor's HR strategy.

Second, it will provide clarity, understanding, and agreement amongst HR team members regarding each one's role, responsibilities and interdependencies. This exercise will help us become a stronger and closer team that will optimally allocate resources, time, and effort toward what will help the business. This, in and of itself, will boost each team member's commitment, inspiration, drive, and eagerness to success.

In the following sections, we will:

- Briefly describe the different phases of the project
- Provide a consolidation of business input
- Propose a global framework that demonstrates the interrelations between business goals and challenges and the way HR can contribute to its success
- Elaborate HR strategies and objectives in more details

1. Overview of the Project

The project consisted of contacting the business leaders we support and asking them in a very structured format what their key challenges and needs for support would be in the future, and how they feel HR could best contribute.

Preparation

First, we agreed on the participants who would be actively involved and would play a key role in this project. Within HR, our newly appointed HR Director would be the overall sponsor and owner of the project. She was assisted by an external consultant, who demonstrated significant experience, expertise, and know-how in this field. Other key HR team members contributed to all of the constituent parts of this project. We also agreed on a sample of business leaders we would involve in this project. These business leaders were members of our local management committee, key members of staff, and business leaders representing other divisions that were being serviced and supported by our HR department.

Next we were all trained and acquired additional skills to conduct in-depth interviews, following a specific format and questionnaire. Finally, we set the timelines for the project, and managed to deliver what was agreed upon within the set timeframes and on top of our "normal" and day-to-day activities.

Interviews with Business Leaders

We interviewed 19 business leaders, representing the core entities of our company, a number of international positions located in Belgium, and a couple of corporate representatives. All interviews took place between November 3rd and December 4th. Topics that were covered during those interviews related to key goals and challenges, activities that could gain in efficiency, elements of frustration, development needs, needed support both in general and specifically related to HR, and expectations towards HR activities that we should start doing, stop doing, or improve on.

Analysis and Consolidation of Data

During a feedback day with the HR core team, we exchanged experiences and tried to discover commonalities in the information we gathered during those interviews on multiple topics. A detailed analysis and consolidation then took place and resulted in the below summary of findings.

HR Strategy and Objectives

This report served as starting point to agree on the final outcomes and the major findings generated from the interviews. Translating these ideas into HR strategies and Plans of Actions was the most crucial team activity we engaged in.

Debriefing the Business Leaders

Finally, we presented the results of this entire project to our business leaders, listened again to their input and when needed, fine-tuned the final results.

2. Consolidating Business Leaders' Input

Identification of Key Goals and Challenges

Key goals, strategies, or objectives were the basis for understanding what our business leaders were focusing on, and what they wanted and needed to deliver in the short- and longer-term future. It provided the overall framework that clarified where we were heading, and the overall direction is we need to move in. Challenges illustrated what business leaders thought would make it difficult to achieve the goals, what might stand in the way; they also illustrated what kept them awake at night. Those challenges could later become opportunities, potential issues to tackle that could clear the way to success.

Key Goals

1. Sales, Revenue, Growth

Most business leaders (13 out of 19) mentioned this topic, although sometimes with different wording or emphasis.

- "Get the business back to sustainable year-on-year top-line growth"
- "Increase productivity and efficacy to hit our targets"
- "Revenue growth"
- "Successful launches of new products"
- "Increase sales"
- "Support the business in achieving their targets"
- "Achieve our sales targets"
- "Double digit growth" and "Support the 10% growth target"
- "Making sure the region is able to reach its revenue targets"

2. Influencing the Environment

A number of business leaders clearly demonstrated an external focus, stressing that we could only succeed if we arrived at influencing the environment we operated in.

- "Continue to gain trust and influence the environment"
- "Think about what to do to prevent the current healthcare system from failing; make sure our Health Policy proposal for adapting the healthcare system gets reflected in the arguments of the politicians' programs for the next elections"
- "Protect the innovative industry by overcoming all pricing and reimbursement issues"
- "Change the negative image we and the pharma industry have by choosing the key players to help us do so"
- "Influence the environment by mitigating the risks and seeing the opportunities we have to make a difference"
- "Support my team through five work streams, all linked to the changing environment, customers as enablers, and patient advocacy groups"

3. Providing Added Value to Our Customers

There were multiple suggestions brought forward to achieve this very broad and vaguely-defined objective.

- "Canalize and focus our efforts toward our important customers and jump out as an organization, making sure the customer sees that we are different"
- "Optimize relations with the hospitals as institutions"
- "Demonstrate the added value of medicines, not only in terms of pricing, but in providing appealing rationale and arguments so

that decision-makers will agree to intervene in reimbursement and thus increase access to medication for patients"

- "Develop relations with external parties to create healthy interaction and a clear and established channel to exteriorize our ideas"
- "Develop and implement customer plans for non-traditional customers"
- "Lift the overall professionalism of a number of countries to the level we are used to here"
- "Find innovative ways to create value based upon the risk and trust policy"

4. Implement the new Business Model Internally

Another number of goals related more to our internal functioning, to what we needed to do internally so that we could achieve all of the above-mentioned groups of goals. We would call these goals underlying internal conditions, requirements to make the above happen and visible to the outside world.

- "Live our new business model project"
- "Align with the new model; optimally fulfill our roles within the new framework"
- "Foster the organization through the new model's implementation"
- "Successfully implement the transformation"
- "Collaborate as well as we can with other departments"
- "Increase cross-functional collaboration and alignment/uniformity across departments and sub-departments so that we come out as one team"
- "Deal with changes and impacts on the team due to the creation of cross-section teams"

- "Fill the gap for the 60% of our portfolio that is not supported by the cross-section teams"
- "Consolidate the new hospital business model"
- "Make sure the new European structure will work"

5. Function- or Domain-Specific Goals that Will Support the Overall Goals

A number of goals were rather specific and related to a specific domain of expertise.

- "Make sure to provide the correct set of financial data so that scenarios can be built and correct business decisions can be made"
- "Optimally use the division's scarcer resources"
- "Roll out the new field force support structure without major distortion to the business"
- "Increase operational efficiency through simplification and automatization"
- "Provide innovative systems and create through technical support a win-win situation for the business"
- "Create business opportunities"
- "Obtain correct prices and reimbursement conditions for our products"
- "Align with global processes, tools, and systems so that we minimize time spent on creating things that might not be necessary"

Challenges
Most challenges mentioned related to the implementation of the new business model.

1. New Business Model Challenges

- "Getting the entire organization to act the same way, in line with the new customer approach"
- "Coming out to customers as one single group, in values, in image, in science, and in contacts"
- "Clarifying roles and responsibilities to make the new business model's structure work and live"
- "Creating role clarity within the new teams"
- "Getting appointments with key players to discuss and defend our products and related prices"
- "Introducing outcomes measurement to measure the results of the healthcare system and design adaptations to the current system to better answer the new healthcare needs"
- "Realizing we do not really know our customers or their needs very well, but do not get the time to discuss this properly, since the available time is spent discussing our products"
- "Finding resources to make sure that now that we are visiting our customers, we can answer their needs. By meeting them, we realize we can do so much, but we will not be able to do it all"
- "Finding ways to meet our internal customers who are now going outside, to discuss and develop business opportunities"
- "Lacking in competencies, capabilities, and understanding around the need to change to be successful in this new environment"
- "Preparing people, specifically those with customer-facing activities, for the new organization and helping them develop a number of interpersonal skills"

2. More General Challenges

- "Negative climate: people are nervous, feel threatened, and so focus on themselves andon differentiating themselves from others, which comes in the way of teamwork and customer orientation"

- "Pressure on the organization makes it hard to keep people enthusiastic and engaged"
- "Dealing with a constant sense of urgency"
- "Achieving objectives in a constantly changing environment"
- "Performing and reaching our targets with respect to compliance and in a context of fierce generic competition and volatile systems"
- "Focusing on priorities while at the same time serving smaller divisions"
- "Continuing to provide adequate support with limited resources"
- "Less investment due to cost cutting"
- "Retaining the good people in this constantly changing environment"
- "Attracting and retaining talents"
- "Change in profiles: you need all-round people now who can adapt to individual customers and who have human knowledge to create contacts"
- "Selecting the key people you want to go ahead with, putting the optimal structure in place, and developing them to take all critical positions within the organization"
- "Creating an inspiring climate where everyone is willing and able to give the best of himself"
- "Retaining through talent management valuable people who can convey knowledge to internal and external stakeholders and be genuine ambassadors for our company"
- "Winning the war for talent"
- "Talent development and succession planning"
- "Current short-term focus while ROI is more long-term"
- "Keeping or gaining a better balance between conducting studies that will help our image, reputation, and revenues"

- "Making plans that stick and are proactive, within an almost randomly changing environment"
- "Getting involved early and proactively in projects so that we can participate in strategic thinking"
- "Dependence of pan-European structures and corporate interferences that impose certain programs and prevent you from making your own decisions"
- "Being able to say no to decisions made by corporate for political reasons that hurt the business and that are too short-term focused"

Identification of Efficiency Gains

In this section we discussed what came up when asking questions related to what activities could be done more effectively or differently, what frustrated people, and what kind of general support our business leaders would need. All these elements were brought together because we noticed a number of similarities in the ideas that came back regularly.

Afterwards, we hoped that this would create some guidance on how we could make opportunities out of the challenges mentioned above. Putting it differently, we believed that we could find inspiration to create the conditions that would enable us to turn challenges that might otherwise jeopardize the achievements of our goals into opportunities.

Work Processes and Procedures (Local and US-driven)

1. *Simplification, Fewer Reports and Templates, Fewer Procedures, Less Bureaucracy, Pragmatic Approach*

   - "A stable office environment without too much bureaucracy where people can really focus on things they need to do"
   - "Simplify things and reduce the time we spend in managing certain systems too often installed to control extremes and exceptions"

- "Simplify brand and customer planning and strategic planning: we plan too much but forget to execute, so we need to replan because the results are not there"
- "Simplify and reduce bureaucracy and standardization"
- "Huge bureaucracy"
- "Install a more pragmatic approach to deal with things, stop firefighting, step back and understand where the fire came from"
- "Learn to accept and live with something that is maybe not 100% correct"
- "We are *the* template factory"
- "People seem to be paid to change templates and ask the same thing over and over again, but in different formats"
- "Useless work that increases workload and does not serve anything"
- "Stop duplicating things; reports in two or three different ways do not add any value"
- "Too many procedures, and need to go through lots of meetings to get everybody's input prior to changing it"
- "Stop making things so complex"
- "Heavy and long processes that require a lot of effort and input"
- "Too many procedures that kill all creativity"

2. *Fewer Meetings*

- "Reduce the number of meetings;, we request too much input from everybody, we take teamwork too literally and spend too much time discussing and meeting"
- "Avoid team discussions sometimes: decide what needs a team discussion and what doesn't"
- "Reduce number of meetings; asking input and stimulating teamwork must happen in other ways as well; we've moved too far in our consensus climate; we should extract input from the organization in other ways"

- "Too many meetings where you ask yourself why you are participating, and it generates a giant workload"
- "Working effectively together without increasing the number of meetings"

3. *Speed Up Decision-making*

- "Decision platforms should speed up making decisions and giving approvals"
- "Too slow in making decisions"
- "Simplify things so we can make decisions faster without involving the whole company"
- "Decisions take too long"
- "We should act like a small company"

4. *Head Office Control*

- "Freedom to operate so that Head Office stops treating us like children and lets us run our business"
- "No empowerment, Head Office needs to control and verify everything without understanding it properly"
- "We do not get the authority to make decisions"
- "We hire intelligent people, we are closest to the market, why should we not make the decision"

Short-term Focus and Constant Change

- "Stop changing scope and contents of projects"
- "Acceleration of change and centralization creates unclarity"
- "Let us implement and execute our plans"

- "Short-term strategy; we can only realize added value if there is some stability so that projects can provide ROI, which is impossible if systems change all the time"
- "Everything needs to be done now"
- "Constant changes: you never see the results of what was planned because we're forced to change it again"

Structure and Alignment

- "Getting the optimal organizational structure and business model operational, allowing sufficient freedom in the market to decide on certain parameters based upon good benchmarking data"
- "Support from other departments to set key priorities instead of trying to do too much"
- "Better alignment between different plans and different departments within the country and within Europe"
- "Aligning processes across divisions and between local and European HR"
- "Stronger alignment between what we do and what we do in the affiliates in the countries"
- "Put the European matrix structure in place with clear processes, roles, and responsibilities and with a compromise in centralization and delocalization so that we can use country specifics as a richness"
- "Become involved early on in consultation meetings and structured ways of information sharing"
- "More effective communication so that issues can be raised and treated early"
- "Discipline to stick to what has been said and agreed upon"

Resources: Headcount and Financial

- "We need more dedicated headcount from within the politics environment, to strengthen our public effort to visit politicians to show and explain the added value of pharma, and to do something about this profound lack of knowledge"
- "We need more people to absorb more"
- "We need sufficient headcount to answer the needs of our customers"
- "Find the most effective way of using available resources across sites"
- "Competent people with the right set of capabilities and long-term commitment so that continuity is taken care of"
- "Financial support"
- "Support in how we can do more with less resources"
- "Logistical support"

Motivate and Retain

1. *Reward and Recognition Programs*

- "Create more visibility for people behind the screens and demonstrate the value they bring"
- "Supporting departments receive too little valorization and recognition for what they do"
- "No genuine recognition of people; we should recognize on more grounds than just sales targets"

2. *Working Conditions: Work-life Balance*

- "HR needs to create the conditions of a really beneficial competitive advantage, with room for flexible working that will attract people to join us and that will ensure they will not bother working during the weekend since they get sufficient reward instead"

- "Find ways to keep the pressure on our people bearable so that there is a perceived work-life balance"
- "Develop strategies to deal creatively with new needs in terms of work-life balance that the new generation puts forward, and that even older people start to pronounce"

3. *Compensation and Benefits*

- "A highly motivated office environment ensures we can retain our talents through a strong long-term incentive plan, offering packages that are much more attractive than they are now"
- "Our philosophy is too old-fashioned; we need to get away from talking about midpoints and we need to push the envelope"
- "Revisit the incentive plans, rating system, and associated salary increases"
- "We need to offer correct and competitive packages"

- "My personal opinion, in times like this: while struggling going through this transformation, people do not get their bonuses, there are less salary increases, and rewards are flattening out. I think we should pay people more, because now we should retain people, we have money, and it would stimulate people to get through this situation"

4. *Involvement, Communication, Information, Individualization*

- "Motivating and retaining people by showing them the future picture, showing them the light at the end of the tunnel, involving them in the process so they stay on track, and showing them results along the way, bringing successes to the forefront"

- "We've become less involved then we used to; our role in proactive planning and strategic thinking has been reduced to more executing and operational stuff"
- "Understanding differences, managing exceptions instead of taking into consideration only the middle of the Gauss curve: stop management of the means"
- "Richness of a company is not over democracy, but understanding that people and departments are different. Unfortunately, in our company, the Gauss curve rules and both extremes are cut off"
- "Make sure people can really speak up frankly"

Develop

- "Training at all levels, from product-related to coaching"
- "Increase our people's quality"
- "Training and support to develop the new business model"
- "Develop skills to interact with customers, interact with strong spokespersons in the country"
- "Training and development, not merely web-based but also interpersonal"
- "Development of skills so that my people can establish a more external focus: languages, communication skills"
- "HR should play a big role in helping us really manage people through current times that imply less resources, new people, new positions, new bosses"
- "Coaching and people management taking into consideration the individual, truly listening to people, showing interest in people, and demonstrating human warmth"

HR Expectations

Having gained a better insight into the most important business goals, the challenges our business leaders face in achieving them, and the obstacles they see, we narrowed down the discussion to HR and the role HR should play in helping them achieve these goals. This was discussed in terms of specific HR support, HR's key objectives, and what HR should stop doing, continue to do, should improve upon, and should start doing.

To Stop Doing

All of our business leaders were very short in this section; they did not really see much that needed to stop, and there were only a few things mentioned. **Eldorado**[5] was mentioned several times as something that did not really demonstrate much added value and totally missed its purpose.

- "Eldorado does not feel like it's being very effective or helping us a lot; we'd rather have some *limited* number of personalized services, like childcare during holidays, or a fitness room in the office. Eldorado is a nice to have, but it does not change one's life."
- "Being an Employer of Choice means standing out and offering more fancy and customized things; so far we outsource this completely like with Eldorado, so it loses all personal touch."
- "I do not see much added value in Eldorado, I've never used it myself"
- "We need to know what people are concerned about, what keeps them with us, and it certainly will not be Eldorado—this keeps me and others 'empirically cold'"

The IIP (Immediate Improvement Plan) and PIP (Performance Improvement Plan) process/procedure was the second "winner" with a lot of votes for dismantling. It was not the fact that we should stop managing low performers, but those interviewed felt changes were needed.

---

[5] Eldorado is a dummy name for an organization our company works with to offer a set of comfort services to our employees (e.g., babysitting, ironing services, product discounts, free tickets for events, etc.)

- "Simplify the process"
- "Stop spending too much time on low performers and don't turn this into a Chinese torture prior to making a decision to separate"
- "This whole IIP and PIP stuff, we should solve this by making it an integral part of the coaching process"

Finally, the concept of **standardized development** was also mentioned, more specifically the idea of stopping the standard procedure of having a development plan in place for each and every individual, and having standard programs for all, obliging people to develop.

- "I do have questions related to the development programs we have installed just because we want to do development for employees. I do not think these are always thought through and there is not really a certainty that it will link the employee to us"
- "What's been done in the development area is poor; it's easy to provide trainings and give people a booklet to choose from, but this is not providing development in my perception"
- "We follow the process related to development, sending people to Insead, etc., but some people do not want to be developed, they want to be left alone. We should let these people do their jobs if they do it well and not bother them and their managers with the obligation to write something down at year-end related to development: this is a complete waste of time, searching for development when they do not want it or see the added value of it"

To Continue Doing

The business leaders were very clear and anonymous in what we should continue doing. In nine interviews, the **HR business partnering**/HR Single Point Of Contact/HR generalist approach was mentioned as something very valuable and important.

- "The generalist approach: have someone I can come to that makes me as an employee feel supported and taken care of"
- "Continue the operational support in case of issues or problems"
- "In the past, HR has been a weak point, but I saw the willingness to change that, to be a real business partner. I need HR as a neutral source, where it works cross-functionally, is not biased, and can be used as a temperature check for the organization"
- "The support HR generalists provide is excellent"

However, as you will read below, there was improvement possible and necessary within this area. All the more "basic stuff" like **paying our salaries** was of course mentioned, sometimes in a humoristic way. Finally, in three instances, the current **recruitment process** was highlighted as having improved a lot, with a streamlined process that reduces the amount of work the business has to do.

To Improve Upon or Begin Doing

1. *Business Understanding, Business Partnering*

What clearly came out was the need to demonstrate a better understanding of the business, of the way our business leaders operated, and of the issues they dealt with. This implied a need for the HR Department being closer to the business, being more visible and accessible, and thinking with them about possible improvements or solutions to their concerns.

- "HR needs to go out into the organization, meet the customers and show them in words and actions what you can do for them"
- "Increase your understanding of our business, profiles we need, and processes we use"

- "Be closer to people, be part of them, assist in meetings, make sure people get more direct access to HR; people need to know and see you so they feel you'll listen and can be trusted"
- "Better understanding and feel of the business, live the operational life"
- "Be closer to your customers, take the time to attend meetings, listen to them, understand what they are doing, be out there, walk around"
- "Know more about the business, the products, be a part of business discussions"
- "Participate every six to eight weeks in our departmental meeting, which will generate an opportunity to raise HR issues"
- "Be more proactive instead of being called upon in case of a problem"
- "Think with us, act proactively, come to see your business and tell us what you've been thinking about related to *xyz*, e.g., CRO's, helping us find ways to better deal with empty territories"
- "Facilitate departmental workshops at department's requests"
- "Market yourself: let us know what you can all do"

2. Revisit and Simplify HR Processes, Procedures, and Practices

On a number of occasions, this was mentioned in the broad sense as above, sometimes regarding the need for increased flexibility and pragmatism in dealing with issues instead of following the rules. A number of times, people went more into specifics. Below are the topics they were thinking about in terms of reviewing and simplifying,

- Performance management process
- Management of low performers: spending less time on low performers, and redirecting this energy toward paying specific attention to high performers, or at least finding a better balance between both aspects

- Review the rating process and system and its link to pay increases: find ways to differentiate more clearly
- Review the salary scales for sales representatives and develop a linear pay curve
- Give the business the power to manage for their own people the salary increase budget
- Review the internal promotion policy (linked to assigning, posting, assessments)
- Simplify the drug reimbursement policy for employees
- Review the car policy
- Review and simplify the mobile phone policy
- Play a role in the 360° process
- Integrate local and Head Office HR processes
- Review the website

3. Create the Best Working Conditions in a Human Climate

We needed to make sure our organization was a good employer; moreover, we desired to be the Employer of Choice so we could attract better candidates, and make our current employees happy to encourage performance and retention. A number of quotes illustrate the great scope of this topic.

- "Define what an Employer of Choice really is and looks like, and specifically what it means for the younger population and the younger generations"
- "We need to do something about the societal phenomenon that younger people have a different attitude and way of looking at their professional lives than we do. We cannot ignore this trend and are not strong enough to go against it, so we need to find creative ways to integrate this trend in our way of doing business with people. If we cannot find a sufficient answer to these new needs, in terms of keeping the pressure bearable and in terms of

work-life balance, we will lose people and this will not benefit our customers or our continuity. Amongst the younger generation, a work-life balance has become a prerequisite to join or stay with a company, but this is also starting to play its role amongst 'older' generations"

- "We need to stand out as an organization and this means developing fancy things like massage buses and bicycle teams, and doing this ourselves without outsourcing it"

- "We need to create a climate where people really feel at home and have primary and secondary conditions that are second to none"

- "We need to come up with creative ways to differentiate ourselves as an employer from the competition. We are a bread-and-butter company: We do what everybody else does, so we need creativity in developing new strategies and opportunities to get employees to join us, so they get the 'wow' reaction ('my organization really understands me, is with me, does great things for me')"

- "We need to think about flexible working, need to consider part-time work for a number of positions and get rid of the resistance against it"

- "We need to bring people together socially, develop initiatives that will create emotional bonds, make sure there are human interactions and exchanges, create warmth, and work on a fraternal atmosphere"

- "We should have personal career counsellors or personal advisors who take care of all the day-to-day concerns people have. It's like when you have a bank, you set up an account, and next the banker advises you where to invest your money. People need to feel and see that they are taken care of"

- "HR should treat both the collectivity and the individual"

- "Our organization and HR need a softer image, a shoulder to cry on"

- "The current image HR has is of a department that provides technical services. The H has gone missing"
- "HR needs to gain trust, just like we need from the outside customers, and this will only happen if you go out there, get to know each other and demonstrate what you can do"

4. *Talent Planning, Talent Management – Succession Planning*

This topic was mentioned in general terms five times. Below are two sample quotes giving more detail.

- "We should take a very good look at talent planning, what it is and how we should best do it, because filling sheets once a year, and locking it in a drawer, is not the way it works. Sometimes talent planning is no more than a buzzword with little content"
- "There is no doubt about it that the whole notion of talent management is very critical, but we've never seen it function properly"

On top of this, the following quotes illustrated what our business leaders needed related to this topic.

- "We need to have insight in our talents so that when we have vacancies, we can assign people directly instead of posting and already knowing who we want there—this is not fair and a waste of time"
- "Talent management: We had a talent review two years ago, and I haven't seen anything since; we do not know where our talents are and do not follow them up closely enough"
- "Talent management: Identify, coach, follow up regarding talents. There is a lot to do at all levels of the organization. There is no coaching of talents. I still cannot understand why it is so difficult

to have a 'portrait' made by an external party, so that I can have an idea of my potential"

- "Talents have been identified: there must be some objective way to picture them"
- "If we could have these kind of assessments and clear pictures of our talents, we would know up front who to assign to what position so that when a position becomes vacant, we can act immediately and make a decision based upon strong, objective information and data. It will help with succession planning efforts and decision-making. The fact that expectations might be created must be more than manageable"
- "Talent development needs to help pushing colleagues to increase flexibility in their thinking about careers. People do not automatically think of opportunities that are not directly 'within their box' or linear career path"

Succession planning was mentioned five times, in general terms of installing this process, but also in personal terms ("preparing my succession") and in terms of "bringing this down to the level of lower management."

5. *Development*

In a number of interviews this topic was put on the table in terms of development of employees, and not just limited to talents.

- "We should provide possibilities to develop people"
- "We should move into personalized training and development, and not picking it from a booklet"
- "We should start with development in line with specific typologies of people, or target groups that have similar needs, and then provide personalized answers to it (e.g., there must be

multiple 55+ who do not know how to efficiently use their PC, so providing them with a standard excel training will not help)"
- "There are people who need specific development to allow them to job rotate"

The need for coaching was also clearly mentioned.

- "Coaching managers in dealing with low performers every step of the way"
- "Coaching people on how to set up a development plan, how to implement and execute it, and following it up"
- "Coaching managers in dealing with their people in these difficult times"

During the interviews, we also focused two specific questions on the development needs our business leaders identified related specifically to their team members and/or to themselves. Three important topics came out of this questioning.

1. **People Management and Coaching**

2. **Customer Behavior**
   - Learn to identify and understand customers' needs
   - Develop the skills and competencies to demonstrate customer-focused behavior
   - Create an external focus

3. **Communication**
   - Communication in interpersonal relations
   - Transferring technical knowledge
   - Languages

HR's Key Objectives

Taking all of the above into consideration, the key objectives that were mentioned should been a logical consequence. Fortunately, they were.

1. **Talent Management** in the broad sense of the word (from attracting top talents to developing them and providing career opportunities)
   - Attract top talent, have the best pharma people with us
   - Talent management
   - Have the right people in the right place with the right skills
   - Training and development of people
   - Provide and develop career opportunities

2. **Create the Best Climate**
   - Employer of Choice
   - Make people proud to work for this organization
   - Create a pleasant environment with a manageable pressure and human way of doing things
   - Women-friendly environment (home working, work-life balance, part-time flex)
   - Part-time flexibility
   - Facilitate human exchange and contact

3. **Retain People**

4. **Business Partner**
   - Support the business
   - Be close, informal
   - Change agent, driving the transformation
   - Be part of the business

3. Global Framework: HR's Role in Supporting the Business

Summary of Our Thinking and translation to our future model

A comprehensive overview of what the business needs to achieve, what major challenges our business faced, and the ideas related to the ways HR can contribute in achieving these goals led us to the next step.

We took a helicopter view, trying to discover how things stuck together, what interdependencies we saw, and how we could deduct from this the primary focuses and strategies HR should develop to finally significantly and positively define a company-original HR, positively influencing the achievement of our business goals. Here is the proposal starting from the key business strategies, translating into HR:

Our company's primary—almost only—overriding goal s **growth and revenue**. Although it was not discussed during the interviews, the reason why we need to achieve growth and revenue lies in our mission: "Passion for your Health." Our company eventually wants to participate in creating a healthier world.

Growing and hitting our revenue targets has become extremely difficult due to all the external changes in the environment. So the objective of growing and gaining revenue, in and of itself, given the context we are facing, is a major challenge.

We can only achieve this if we can "promote" innovative medicines, and the innovative pharmaceutical industry. We need to advocate for and protect our industry, and create access to innovative medication for patients and citizens. If not, we will not be able to sell, and thus we will not gain revenue and will not grow. If we do not have sufficient revenue, we will no longer have the means to develop new medicines and thus will eventually not be able to contribute to society's health.

Protecting and promoting our medicines and our innovative industry means we need to **influence the current Healthcare System**. This is only possible if we can influence and convince those who create and direct the

Healthcare System, **the Healthcare stakeholders**. The only way we will be able to convince them of the absolute necessity to protect and promote the innovative industry and thus adapt the current Healthcare System is by **making them trust us**. They need to trust us, they need to value us and recognize us, so they will come to understand that what we want to accomplish by influencing them and the system serves a much higher goal than merely making profit. It will eventually serve society and human health.

The Healthcare Stakeholders will only value and recognize us in our true and genuine value if we change their perception of us, if we **reverse our current image**. And changing our image into a positive one can be achieved by focusing on their needs and shifting their perception. It implies installing and exteriorizing a true customer-oriented approach— we need to **stand out as a genuine CFO, or Customer-Focused Organization** (rather than a PFO, or Profit-Focused Organization).

If we stand out as an organization by acting upon what they need, their perception of us will change in a positive way; they will start trusting us, and accepting us as a partner that has a valuable and authentic voice. They will have ears for our points of view in the healthcare reform debate and we will be able to convince them to change the system. If they change the system in a way that allows innovative drugs to be supported and promoted, they will increase access to those medicines for patients, so that we can eventually grow and have sufficient revenues to continue developing new drugs, thus positively influencing the overall health of society.

Let's now take it a step further.

How can we become an organization that stands out to our external stakeholders? How can we truly be seen as a customer-oriented and customer-focused organization? We can achieve this if and only if we **jump out from within**. This means we need to act, work, and be seen as a customer-focused entity, so we need to influence, change, and **evolve into a new business model** (CFO), a new system (cf. the analogy to influencing the healthcare system), and a way of interacting with our customers.

A system, business model, or organization can only work and function successfully if we can **influence the stakeholders** that make it work. This time, we refer to those stakeholders that will be able to implement this business model: our employees. And the only way to influence them is by **making them trust us**. Employees, our internal stakeholders, need to trust our organization, need to value our company and recognize it for what it does and how it does it.

Gaining the employees' trust means changing their perception of us, moving toward a **positive, trustworthy image**. And this can be accomplished if we grow into an **Employee-Focused Organization**: an EFO! (Note that in fact this is nothing more than a CFO, but applied to a specific type of customers, our internal customers, our employees.)

And what will this be like? An Employee-Focused Organization? **An EFO is an organization that creates all primary and secondary conditions that will make it stand out as the best employer**, the employer of choice, second to none. It will no longer be "the bread and butter company" (the company that does what every other company does and provides), but "the caviar company" (the company that goes that extra mile, that differentiates itself, and that values in words and actions every single individual for its crucial role in the whole of a CFO).

What then can we distillate as being primary and secondary conditions for this particular company? If we know this, and we can create the very best of those conditions, we will gain trust from our internal stakeholders around the new business model put in place, and they will make it work. This will then be noticed by our external customers, who will also start trusting us, seeing us as a valuable partner to discuss and review the healthcare system with, thus safeguarding the future of innovative medicines and of our company.

We can define **primary conditions** as those elementary conditions that will make our company as an EFO different from the others. Primary conditions are conditions linked to the individual employee, conditions that will eventually make them **willing and capable** of implementing and living the CFO. These conditions will make our internal stakeholders—our employees—feel at home, comfortable, taken care of, happy, enthusiastic, committed, engaged, and capable to perform.

The primary conditions are twofold. One set is linked to the **individual's perception of the work environment**, and the way people are taken care of. This is what makes them willing. This refers to the company-original definition and application of what constitutes an Employer of Choice for them, i.e. work-life balance, a pleasant environment to work in, human contact and exchange, personal counseling, recognition and rewards, individual approach, initiatives that create emotional bonds, etc.

The other set of primary conditions is linked to the **individual skills and competencies**: all activities an organization initiates and supports that will make them capable. This relates to everything that links into **talent management**: having the right people in the right place with the right skills, developing them to perform and to grow, assessing their potential, providing career tracks—ensuring our employees have or develop the capabilities they need to perform in the positions that best match their abilities.

But having the people willing, committed, happy (resulting from attractive primary working conditions), and capable of performing (linked to primary capability conditions), will only lead to maximum performance and maximum overall satisfaction if the **work processes and procedures** ultimately support and enable this. These enablers, or **secondary conditions,** are inherent to the way work is being organized. It refers to simplification of processes, reduction of bureaucracy and duplication, empowerment, procedures that help instead of hinder performance—in other words, overall best practices for doing business and getting things done.

Underlying all of this is the role we ask the employees to fulfill, sometimes implicitly, sometimes explicitly, to help change the business, change the people that make the business, **change the organization**, and provide support in getting everyone through this process.

This leads us then to what HR should focus on when revamping its department and practices. Given the above rationale, HR should focus on creating the primary and secondary conditions by:

- Installing a human, personal, and personalized employee focused climate reflecting the Employer of Choice concept: WILLING
- Providing the employees with the means to perform well through extensive talent planning, management, and development: CAPABLE
- Creating and reinforcing the business processes and embracing change that will enable the employees to perform at their maximum potential: ENABLED

If HR can achieve this, we will be able to retain a highly motivated, capable and enabled workforce, we will become an **Employee-Focused Organization,** and we will stand out in the way we take care of and manage our "human capital."

Returning to our Case Study, when we reviewed what our business leaders put forward as **key HR objectives,** we could see that they were very much in line with the above conclusion regarding primary and secondary conditions.

C A P A B L E	**1. Talent Management** in the broad sense of the word (from attracting top talents, to developing them and providing career opportunities) • Attract top talent, have the best pharma people with us • Talent management • Have the right people in the right place with the right skills • Training and development of people • Provide and develop career opportunities

2. Create the Best Climate

- Employer of Choice
- Make people proud to work here
- Create a pleasant environment with manageable pressure and a human way of doing things
- Create a women-friendly environment (home working, work-life balance, part-time flex)
- Offer part-time flexibility
- Facilitate human exchange and contact
- Manage our human capital

3. Retain People

4. Business Partner

- Support the business, be part of the business
- Be close, informal
- Change agent, driving the transformation

Our Thinking Visualized

Below, you can see visually how we summarized all of the above thinking into a company-original HR that will help us stand out and generate genuine impact on our business. It is embedded in the new strategic framework (Customer-Focused Organization) and offers a roadmap for implementation through the identification of key HR objectives.

CFO implies EFO

EFO is an inherent part of CFO: if we fully live
CFO, we will act towards our employees as
our customers, and by making explicit that
our C is E, we come to an EFO

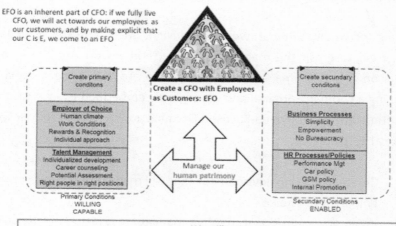

Create primary conditons	Create a CFO with Employees as Customers: EFO	Create secondary conditons
Employer of Choice Human climate Work Conditions Rewards & Recognition Individual approach		**Business Processes** Simplicity Empowerment No Bureaucracy
Talent Management Individualized development Career counseling Potential Assessment Right people in right positions	Manage our human patrimony	**HR Processes/Policies** Performance Mgt Car policy GSM policy Internal Promotion
Primary Conditions WILLING CAPABLE		Secundary Conditions ENABLED

We will

Retain a highly motivated **willing, capable and enabled** workforce

4. Elaboration of HR Strategies and Goals

During our two-day seminar, we gained insight into the business leaders' input, tried to grasp the magnitude, scope, and HR potential in it, and agreed on the outcome as described above. To meet the criteria of becoming a company-original and strategically embedded HR, we focused on shifting into an Employee-Focused Organization by achieving following four key HR strategies:

1. Create a working environment that will make us a recognized Employer of Choice
2. Implement individualized talent management (attract, develop and retain)
3. Take the lead in simplifying HR tools and processes, making them more effective and easy to use
4. Act as a change and transformation agent for the organization and for the employees

Next, we took each of these four strategies and brainstormed on all the things we could/should do to implement them, always taking into consideration examples and ideas we received from our business leaders.

Key Strategy 1: Create a Working Environment that Will Make Us a Recognized Employer of Choice

The achievement of this goal requires actions in a number of defined fields and categories. We identified actions, initiatives, and activities that can be linked to:
   a) the social environment
   b) rewards and recognitions
   c) promoting and developing specific behaviors
   d) infrastructure
   e) work/life balance

Key Strategy 2: Implement Individualized Talent Management (attract, develop and retain)

This goal reflects what was mentioned frequently: put the right man in the right place at the right time. In brainstorming on this topic, we discovered a number of categories of activities to launch. Taking into consideration the emphasis that was put on it, as well as our current experiences in losing valuable people and having difficulties in finding new talents, this will become one of our short-term priorities:

a) Attract talents
b) Identify key and emerging talents
c) Develop and deploy key and emerging talents
d) Develop all people
e) Performance management for all
f) Retention of talents

Key Strategy 3: Take the Lead in Simplifying HR Tools and Processes, Making These more Effectively and Easy to Use

Below is a list of HR processes, procedures and tools to simplify that were mentioned by our business leaders.

a) Performance management and performance improvement
b) Compensation and benefits policies
c) HR communication process, tools, channels
d) Internal promotions process
e) Vacancy management process

Key Strategy 4: Act as a Change and Transition Agent for the Organization and the Employees

Finally, activities and actions linked to our not-fully-defined but definitely identified role as change and transition agent in the transformation and change processes are listed below.

a) Gain change management capability
b) Coaching of change agents
c) Change related communication strategy

GET YOUR FREE RESOURCE

A very useful and unique tool, the Interview Protocol, comes with this book as a free bonus. To make sure you get the most benefit from this book, download the extra tool using the link below:

Standout HR Free bonus

How do you feel about this book, *Standout HR* ?

Thank you for having taken the time to go through my very first published book, *Standout HR*. There are so many good sources available depending upon what you are looking for and how you define your search. I hope the book lived up to your expectations. I hope you found what you were looking for, and more. I hope you felt, most of all, the passion I feel every single day in doing whatever I can to make HR stand out in any company, to the benefit of all human beings.

I would love to hear from you, learn from your feedback to improve what I am doing, or to direct me toward the topics most dear to you to elaborate on in any future books. If you have found value in my book, please spread the word and share your experience with friends, family, and colleagues. If you would like to help other people decide whether this book was worth the purchase, please leave a review on Amazon.

If I can be of any help in other issues, problems, or opportunities you may be facing, do not hesitate to contact me. I wish you all the best in your future success!

Kindest regards,
Veronique Vanmiddelem
Vero.vanmiddelem@gmail.com

ABOUT
VERONIQUE VANMIDDELEM

Veronique Vanmiddelem is an organizational psychologist, with additional credentials in human resources management and change management. Her entire professional career has been built around making people feel good in the environment where they spend most of their time: their workplace. She adopts a helicopter view in discovering the key defining principles of any organization to synchronize with the company HR strategy. In doing so, she shows genuine concern and empathy with both business leaders and their business endeavors, combined with the employees and their energy, talents and skills to build lasting success.

Veronique Vanmiddelem has gained her expertise spending more than 25 years in multiple organizations, local and global, small and big, nonprofit and for profit. Her full profile is available on LinkedIn, feel free to use this link to check out her experiences and expertise. She is now CEO of her own coaching and consulting firm, 3E CnC.

Made in the USA
Monee, IL
24 April 2021